Toward Excellence in Gifted Education

D

Toward Excellence in Gifted Education

John Feldhusen, Editor
Purdue University

Contributors:

Leland Baska, *Chicago Public Schools*
John Feldhusen, *Purdue University*
William Foster, *Rutgers University*
Ken Seeley, *University of Denver*
Joyce VanTassel-Baska, *Northwestern University*
Grayson Wheatley, *Purdue University*

LOVE PUBLISHING COMPANY
Denver/London

Internal design and typesetting by Special Press, Columbus,
Ohio.

Copyright © 1985 Love Publishing Company
Printed in the United States of America
ISBN 0-89108-150-X
Library of Congress Catalog Card Number 84-80394

Contents

6 Key Administrative Concepts in Gifted Program Development   85
Joyce VanTassel-Baska, Northwestern University

7 Facilitators for Gifted Learners   105
Ken Seeley, University of Denver

⑧ Helping a Child Toward Individual Excellence   135

William Foster, Rutgers University

Illustrations

Preface

This book is a product of the efforts of six people to set their minds in order concerning the nature of giftedness and education of the gifted. We did not originally set out to write a book. We simply came together to puzzle through this complicated field. We decided to meet weekends two or three times a year at stimulating sites and to discipline ourselves to spend at least 16 hours each weekend analyzing and synthesizing our understanding of the gifted.

Thus, it all began at the Keystone resort in the Colorado mountains, with side trips to Chicago and Galena, Illinois. The culmination of our thinking is presented in these chapters, each of which is written by one or two of us.

We have all read and discussed these chapters. Sometimes we battled for hours, but generally we arrived at a reasonable agreement. Then we left the chapter author to create the final version. As a result, there might be some slight contradictions from chapter to chapter. But by and large we believe that we have presented a relatively consistent point of view.

During the years that these ideas were germinating, we were all working in the field of gifted education. All of us had substantial interactions with gifted and talented students, with teachers of the gifted, and with the students' parents. School programs were growing up all over the United States. We were all able to work with or observe a wide variety of program and curriculum models. Those experiences provide much of the motivation for this book.

We are particularly concerned that the ubiquitous pullout/ resource room model, with the frequently disjointed creativity and problem-solving games as the curriculum and "research projects" as the major activity, has come to dominate the field. We believe that the major or first order need of gifted youth is to be able to learn basic skills and concepts in subject matter or disciplines at a pace and level that match the individual's talents and abilities. Rarely is this need even addressed in pullout/resource room programs. It is a major concern of this book.

Gifted youth have other needs as well. They need the opportunity to extend their knowledge through the study of interrelated areas of knowledge. They should experience the discipline of learning at least one language other than their native tongue. They need special forms of career education. They need to achieve better self understanding. These and other needs are described in this book, and we suggest ways to meet these needs through appropriate curriculum and instruction.

Above all, we hope that this book will stimulate practitioners in gifted education to consider carefully the rationale for their programs, for the identification procedures, for the curriculum, and for the overall goals. If readers disagree with our concepts, this will bother us little if they will consider our ideas carefully and offer alternatives that represent still better thinking about how best to educate gifted and talented youth.

1

An Introduction

John Feldhusen

Ultimately, the goal for the gifted and talented, and of our efforts to help them, is to develop a sense of the pursuit of excellence in all performances and endeavors. Along the way the gifted and talented have to acquire special competencies in a particular field of endeavor, they must become generally well educated, they must become motivated to create, and they must achieve self actualization. The criterion of evaluation for all endeavors in the lives of the gifted and talented, however, must be excellence. Gestalt psychology long ago proposed the concept of the "good gestalt," a personal, perceptual model of the ideal accomplishment of a goal. For the gifted and talented, a standard or model of the ideal goal, performance, or product should guide all efforts and become a dominant force in the life of the gifted and talented individual.

The pursuit of excellence is applicable to all fields of human endeavor. It can characterize the evaluative criterion to which Arthur Ashe would strive on the tennis court, Jonas Salk would strive in the laboratory, or Richard Burton would strive on stage. There are different criterion levels within any one area of human endeavor. Thus, an artistically gifted child may strive for a level of excellence defined by other talented people in his or her community, and Van Cliburn strove for the ultimate level of excellence in piano artistry when he entered the Tchaikovsky competition in Moscow. Similarly, Olympic athletes strive to achieve a criterion of excellence at the highest level.

Any society will benefit from developing young people whose level of excellence is expressed at the local level (e.g., an excellent physician, a community theatre director, a superb golfer), the state level, or even nationally, but who do not rise to international fame or eminence. The field of education of the gifted has often seemed to imply that suitable realization of potential talent is to achieve national or international recognition. In truth, society needs the gifted and talented at all levels of leadership and participation. Of course, those who are not gifted or talented may also make significant contributions to their communities through a variety of social, political, and occupational roles performed competently.

THE SENSE OF EXCELLENCE

The sense of excellence grows in a myriad of ways in the gifted and talented. The initial sense, if not pursuit, of excellence derives in large part from experiences in the family and with family members. It stems from seeing high quality artistic or athletic performances, having parents who show enthusiasm for scientific or other scholarly achievements or who model the quest for excellence in their own artistic or professional endeavors, and exposure to older brothers and sisters who already have set goals at a criterion level of excellence. In school opportunities arise to observe gifted teachers and peers who can serve as models, to read biographies and autobiographies of gifted models, to be taught explicit standards of evaluation for excellence in a field of specialization, and to undertake projects whose outcomes can be evaluated for excellence.

Intrinsic Motivation

Gradually the external models of excellence give way to internalized motivations to achieve and to strive for excellence. Intrinsic motivation becomes the dominant force at an early age in gifted and talented youth who will achieve excellence. Thus, the quest for excellence can and must come to characterize the behavior of the gifted and talented. The quest begins in childhood and grows through adolescence into young adulthood as the standards of excellence become more and more clearly articulated through knowledge of a field of specialization and the standards of excellence in that field. This striving for excellence, combined with the desire to create, to solve, to innovate, to produce, becomes the guiding motivation of the gifted and talented.

Static or Dynamic?

Giftedness and talent are too often viewed as static and fully developed abilities. If a child is gifted or talented, many people expect him or her to be able to perform at a high level. In reality, giftedness and talent in children are simply *potential*, with no fixed state of talent or ability.

At all times in the life of the child, the cognitive, affective, and motoric structures are in a dynamic state of flux. They are actively being used, and through use they become effectively adaptive (through accommodation or assimilation). The changes that occur in the child's ability to reason, to draw, to sing, or to swim are developmental phenomena that take place constantly. New schemas are continually emerging as patterns for processing cognitively or acting physically. Giftedness, as a developmental phenomenon, is constantly changing, ever increasing, growing.

THE PRINCIPAL DOMAINS OF GIFTEDNESS AND TALENT

As a general theoretical conception, at least four principal domains interact to produce giftedness and talent: high-level ability, self-concept, motivation, and creativity. The four domains represent a conceptual abstraction, for surely productive talent or giftedness may represent almost an infinite set of personal, social, and cultural processes that interact by design and chance to yield superior and innovative products, conceptions, and performances.

Ability

We have known for a long time that some genetic transmission of structures sets limits on the physical, neurological, and psychological functioning of individuals. Nichols' (1978) comprehensive review of the heritability of IQ and other traits, however, concluded that researchers do not agree on the relative influence of heredity and environment on the development of human abilities and talents. Thus, our principal concern should be with exploring the potential development of human capacity cognitively, motorically, and affectively, and not with racial, cultural, or sex differences in ability.

Some individuals do seem to be advantaged neurologically by genetic determination and to enjoy from birth onward a facilitating nurturance from parents and their cultural milieu. Our conception of the neurological advantage focuses on certain cognitive functions that we call abilities. These may be perceptual in nature, and they may reveal a capacity to process information about the world and self and to develop schema or cognitive systems for such processing. Some children develop a schema or system to derive meaning from spoken words and to respond with action to those words before age 1. A few children develop the capacity to comprehend and respond motorically to words in print before age 3. By age 3 some children have a quite large vocabulary that they use to act on the world around them. These children have all developed abilities that will continue to grow and possibly culminate in high-level verbal abilities in adolescence and adulthood. Abilities in mathematical reasoning, artistic talent, and spatial visualization may develop in similar patterns.

Abilities are capacities or potential for receiving and processing information about the world and for generating adaptive actions in response to that world. Intelligence tests measure general intellectual capacity to remember, to understand, to reason. Piagetian tasks such as classical conservation or seriation measure a child's ability to comprehend relationships. Later, the adolescent's capacity to deal with mathematical lattices will be viewed as representative of the ultimate level of cognitive functioning—complex formal operations.

For the gifted and talented we expect high levels of ability, aptitude, or talent, but our assessment is essentially comparative. An IQ of 130 simply means that the child has performed better than 95% of the children taking a test. We can, of course, list the tasks that a child can do on a test and thus have a description of real performance, but ultimately we turn comparative or norm seeking. IQ is really a normative term.

Abilities and talents take many forms. Talent in art depends much on perceptual processes and fine motoric capacities. Conversely, talent in golf, swimming, or tennis may depend chiefly on kinesthetic, perceptual, and gross motor functioning. Whatever the form, we recognize that one major component of giftedness is ability or aptitude that sets limits or offers potential for the development of high-level productivity or performance.

Self-Concept

The self as perceived by the gifted or talented individual seems to exert a dynamic force in the development and use of talents and gifts. Self-concept consists of perceptions and interpretation of self, the ideal self to which one strives, and the perceptions of one's own talent and abilities. In a review of self-concept research, Shavelson, Hubner, and Stanton (1976) concluded that perceptions of self are formed through experience with and interpretations of one's experiences and are influenced by reinforcements, evaluations by other people, and attributions regarding our own behavior. In a more recent review Shavelson and Bolus (1982) suggested that self-concept has seven features: It is organized, multifaceted, hierarchical, and stable; it becomes increasingly multifaceted as the individual develops; it has both descriptive and evaluative dimensions; and it can be differentiated from other psychological constructs such as academic achievement or motivation.

In childhood and adolescence gifted and talented youth may experience periods of doubt, despair, or confusion about self in relation to others because their precocity often makes them appear abnormal or freakish. Other children and adults often give evaluations and feedback that the gifted view negatively. Their strong and precocious interests often lead to a perception of self as "out of step." We would hope that the negative signs are balanced with favorable views of self as competent.

Above all, the gifted and talented must come to view themselves as capable of producing new ideas, products, or conceptions or of being able to produce new solutions to problems. Average and low ability students as adolescents and later as adults see their function in life, to a great extent, as learning from and using the wisdom or products generated by others. They may view themselves as able or barely able to ingest and comprehend the ideas developed by scholars, inventors, or artists. But the gifted and talented must, from an early age, come to a sense or view of self as capable of producing new ideas, new products, new artistic productions or performances. Although scales have been designed to measure self-concept in youth in general, or the gifted in particular, few have addressed the assessment of this sense of creative, productive ability. Nevertheless, it is an observable operation. We can observe the student or adult striving to create and infer that this element of self-concept is present, and we can assess it through interviews.

Self-concept in the gifted and talented increasingly becomes a clear view and understanding of one's own talents and abilities, a sense of one's social and affective relationships with other high ability youth, adolescents, and adults. It also incorporates a sense of satisfaction (short of egotism) with self, with one's abilities, and with one's performances. The gifted and talented should achieve a positive sense of strength in viewing self.

Motivation

Motives are products of many aspects of our lives. They represent goals, objectives, aims—that which arouses behavior, that which gives direction, that which sustains behavior, and that which causes behavior to diminish or cease. Motivation is both external and internal. We are motivated by teachers and parents who offer opportunities, who direct, who encourage, or who admonish us to curtail a line of action or thought.

We are also highly concerned with the internal arousing and directing mechanisms derived from perception, attitudes, emotions, and attributions. The internalized motivation is sometimes referred to as intrinsic motivation, implying that it springs from within the individual's own interests or drives. The intrinsic motivation of gifted students also stems from natural curiosity and a need to explore.

Knowledge is another major contributor to motivation, in its power to generate further interest, curiosity, and inquiry behavior. A child who knows nothing about beetles may have no motivation to study them, as Darwin did. But with a modicum of knowledge of beetles, curiosity may be stimulated, and motivation to study beetles further could lead to a variety of activities.

The growth of skill as the gifted and talented master an area of study also produces an intrinsic form of motivation called *competency motivation* (White, 1959). This is a motivational drive that grows upon successive advances in skill development. Each new skill achievement seems to reinforce an increasing need to achieve. Thus, a generalized achievement motivation grows in the gifted.

Nicholls (1983) distinguished two types of intrinsic motivation—task-involvement and ego-involvement. He stated:

> In task-involvement, learning is more inherently valuable, meaningful or satisfying, and attention is focused on the task and strategies to master it rather than on the self. In ego-involvement, on the other hand, learning is a means to the end of looking smart or looking stupid, and attention is focused on the self.

Gifted and talented youth are likely characterized chiefly by high degrees of task-involvement rather than ego-involvement. Their motivation patterns reflect persistence or carrying through on learning tasks when external reinforcers (extrinsic motivation), ego-related conditions, or competition are not present.

Ball (1977) reported carrying out an extensive factor analysis of a motivation scale administered to a large sample of high school students. Five independent factors emerged from the analysis, two of which clearly reflect the intrinsic motivation of task involvement:

1. Positive orientation toward school learning (which involved persistence, high level of aspiration, positive academic self-concept, and positive feelings about past performance at school).

2. Need for social recognition (seeking positive reinforcement from the teacher, competing academically with classmates in order to be seen by them as doing well in school).

3. Motive to avoid failure (fearing failure, high test anxiety).

4. Curiosity (both epistemic and perceptual).
5. Conformity (working because it is "demanded" by the teacher or by parents or, if relevant, by peer pressures).

Clearly, factors 1 and 4 represent forms of intrinsic motivation.

Bloom's (1982) study of highly successful artists, pianists, sculptors, mathematicians, research neurologists, swimmers, and tennis players revealed competitiveness with peers in the specific talent area as one of the salient characteristics associated with high-level success. Although competition is often viewed as extrinsic and likely to detract from long-range or continuing motivation, in school learning situations its association with high-level creative production in the gifted suggests an altogether different effect. Willingness to work hard, to persist, are associated characteristics reported in the Bloom research. Bloom suggested that success involves:

> ...willingness to work hard to achieve a high standard and *competitiveness* and *determination* to do one's best. [*italics ours*].

We expect high levels of intellectual or artistic motivation in gifted and talented individuals. We expect competitiveness and persistence. We expect them to be motivated to learn, to study hard, to read voraciously, to inquire and question, and to pursue projects for extended periods of time—i.e., task commitment as defined by Renzulli (1978). High levels and unique forms of motivation characterize the gifted and talented.

Creativity

We believe that creative capacity is inevitably a component of giftedness. In a sense, creativity and giftedness are synonymous since the definition of each has a major component in common—the capacity to produce ideas or solutions that are unique, or novel, or unusual, as well as worthwhile and adaptive.

Some definitions of giftedness focus only on intellectual capacity in childhood (Terman, 1925); others focus on a combination of intellectual capacity and creativity (Renzulli, 1978). Of course, it can be argued that creativity emerges only as the well-educated gifted child becomes a young adult with well-integrated knowledge in a discipline, but that conception may represent only a view of creativity in adulthood and not the emerging ability in childhood.

Stein (1974) has suggested that creative behavior is characterized by the concept of novelty that is useful. He suggested that novel behavior can come through problem solving, trial and error, and various other activities. He further argued that creativity should be seen as coming in stages in the developmental process. He pointed out that a massive amount of research has been done on the psychological processes of creativity and on the personal characteristics of creative people. Therefore, we are in a good position to assess creativity as a component of giftedness and to nurture it as a major concern in educational programs for the gifted and talented.

MacKinnon (1978) has offered the best composite portrait of the creatively gifted person, because his research emphasized a holistic approach to understanding the nature and personal characteristics of creative people. The composite picture varies somewhat from field to field (e.g., creative writers versus architects), but commonalities are obvious. Highly creative persons in general were found to be well above average in intellectual capacity. They were also found to be discerning, observant, alert, capable of concentrated attention, and fluent in scanning thought. And they were found to have a wide range of information available in memory. Of particular interest and significance is the finding that creatively gifted individuals are relatively free from repression and suppression as mechanisms for control of impulse and imagery. Thus, creative individuals have greater access to their own conscious and unconscious experiences. MacKinnon summarized the portrait of the creative individual:

> ...it is his high level of effective intelligence, his openness to experience, his freedom from crippling restraints and impoverishing inhibitions, his esthetic sensitivity, his cognitive flexibility, his independence in thought and ac-

tion, his unquestioning commitment to creative endeavor, and his unceasing striving for solutions to the ever more difficult problems that he constantly sets for himself. (p. 186)

An alternative view of creativity emerges from the work of Guilford as represented in the theoretical model of human intelligence called the "structure of intellect" (1967). This view of creativity is analytical, conceiving of creativity as a collection of separate traits or abilities, broadly grouped as a combination of fluency, flexibility, originality, and elaboration. Each of these four is differentiated by both the entering content and the exiting products that result from a creative operation.

Guilford noted that all the operations (cognition, memory, divergent and convergent production, and evaluation) contribute to creative and problem-solving behavior, but he emphasized the unique role of divergent operations:

...it seems to be generally recognized that divergent production contributes most to creative thinking....(p. 290)

We may conclude that some constellation of creative traits and divergent abilities, as well as all the other cognitive operations, contributes to the composite view of creativity as a major component of giftedness. The personal traits and characteristics develop during childhood and adolescence, and the various divergent and convergent abilities emerge through interaction with the world of ideas and experiences. Much of this view of creativity overlaps with the component of ability and talent, particularly the component that traces to the work of Guilford. Creative functioning appears to be complex, involving talents, abilities, personal-social characteristics, values, attitudes, and beliefs. Creative functioning is perhaps the *sine qua non* of giftedness.

SERVICES FOR THE GIFTED

The composite of ability, self-concept, motivation, and creativity yields a concept of quantitative and qualitative differences among gifted and talented individuals. The levels of each component may vary, and we may have a differential or diagnostic view of the elements of giftedness or talent. The highly gifted student may have a high IQ, high artistic capacities, or superior strength and coordination. The self view may reflect an awareness and positive feeling about the strength or capacity. Capacity for innovative thought or problem solving may be high. And from a variety of performance and self-report indicators, we may infer high-level motivation to achieve, to produce, to innovate, to excel.

The highly gifted have diverse needs that require an accelerated and enriched general educational curriculum, a superior specialization curriculum, opportunities to work with peers and adult mentors who provide high level modeling and stimulation to achieve, excel, and create, and a supportive family situation if they remain living at home (Passow, 1979; Feldhusen & Wyman, 1980). Meeting those needs calls for a smorgasbord of experiences and opportunities to learn (Stanley, 1980).

Across the services spectrum the smorgasbord concept implies a related set of opportunities and experiences in and out of school, organized by teachers, parents, and counselors, or in adolescence by the gifted and talented youth themselves. These might be a summer at Interlochen, Saturday classes at Julliard, a summer Governor's school, after-school enrichment classes, a museum program, travel abroad, a library reading program, historical tours, opportunities to work with mentors, college classes while in junior high or high school, and so on. The list is endless. The purpose is to meet both the general educational needs and the specialization needs of the gifted and talented (Feldhusen, 1979).

A program for the gifted and talented is a structured set of experiences, guided by a knowledgeable teacher, which employs appropriate curriculum. Curriculum is the set of ideas (facts, concepts, principles, generalizations, problems) that the student confronts and interacts with in the *generative* learning process. The interaction is dynamic, constructive, and evaluative. From the interaction the gifted student should gain concepts, schema, understanding, skill, and organized knowledge. Our model for a differentiated curriculum stresses (1) acceleration of regular content, (2) rapid pace, (3) examination of issues to greater depth, and whenever possible (4) interdisciplinary investigation to assure broad, holistic understanding. Affective needs and issues of social context should be incorporated into the instruction whenever possible.

SUMMARY

The concept of differential programming to meet the diverse needs and levels of giftedness and talent in youth will be developed and elaborated in a later chapter. The ultimate goal is to help gifted and talented youth acquire a sense of striving for excellence and to facilitate their development to the highest levels in the areas of ability, self-concept, motivation, and creativity. The overall conception recognizes that self-actualization or full functioning in the gifted and talented may be realized at various levels ranging from high-level success locally to international fame or eminence.

REFERENCES

Ball, S. (Ed.). *Motivation in education.* New York: Academic Press, 1977.

Bloom, B.S. The role of gifts and markers in the development of talent. *Exceptional Children,* 1982, *48,* 510-522.

Feldhusen, J.F. Gifted education and the curriculum. *Agenda G/T,* 1979, 3, 1-2.

Feldhusen, J.F., & Wyman, A.R. Super Saturday: Design and implementation of Purdue's special program for gifted children. *Gifted Child Quarterly,* 1980, *4,* 15-21.

Guilford, J.P. *The nature of human intelligence.* New York: McGraw-Hill, 1967.

MacKinnon, D.W. *In search of human effectiveness.* Buffalo, NY: Creative Education Foundation, 1978.

Nicholls, J.G. Conceptions of ability and achievement motivation: A theory and its implications for education. In S.G. Paris, G.M. Olson, & H.W. Stevenson (Eds.), *Learning and motivation in the classroom.* Hillsdale, NJ: Erlbaum, 1983.

Nichols, R.C. Policy implications of the IQ controversy. In L.S. Shulman (Ed.), *Review of research in education* (Vol. 6). Itasca, IL: F.E. Peacock, Publisher, 1978, pp. 3-46.

Passow, A.H. A look around and look ahead. In A.H. Passow (Ed.), *The gifted and the talented: Their education and development* (78th yearbook of the National Society for the Study of Education, Part 1). Chicago: University of Chicago Press, 1979.

Renzulli, J.S. What makes giftedness? *Phi Delta Kappan,* 1978, *60,* 180-184, 261.

Shavelson, R.J., & Bolus, R. Self-concept: The interplay of theory and methods. *Journal of Educational Psychology,* 1982, *74,* 3-17.

Shavelson, R.J., Hubner, J.J., & Stanton, J.C. Self-concept: Validation of construct interpretations. *Review of Educational Research,* 1976, *46,* 407-441.

Stanley, J.C. On educating the gifted. *Educational Researcher,* 1980, *9,* 8-12.

Stein, M.I. *Stimulating creativity* (Vol. 1). New York: Academic Press, 1974.

Terman, L. *Genetic studies of genius: Mental and physical traits of a thousand gifted children* (Vol. 1). Stanford, CA: Stanford University Press, 1925.

White, R.W. Motivation reconsidered: The concept of competence. *Psychological Review,* 1959, *66,* 297-333.

2

A Conception of the Field of Gifted Education

John Feldhusen

At this point we would like to establish a comprehensive framework that will serve as a heuristic to facilitate further research, development, and understanding of gifted and talented students and the nurturance of their abilities. The overall conception will also be used as the framework for analysis and discussions in later chapters of this book. We regard the field of gifted education as nascent but promising as a new area of disciplined inquiry.

Figure 1 presents a visual scheme of the field of gifted education. It suggests four major domains comprising this disciplined area of inquiry: (1) the theoretical bases of the field, (2) program designs and models, (3) the gifted individual, and (4) the facilitators. The four domains operate in concert to yield a comprehensive conception of the process of educating the gifted.

THEORETICAL BASES

The field of gifted education has evolved somewhat around a set of definitions of terms such as *genius, gifted, precocious, creative, talent, ability, intelligence,* and *aptitude.* Each of these terms has a relatively unique but not absolutely fixed meaning in the field of gifted education.

Brief Definitions

"Genius" now refers chiefly to those individuals who have already demonstrated extremely high levels of ability in some meaningful performance, whereas "gifted" commonly denotes a child or adolescent who shows signs or indications of superior ability. "Precocious" describes a child or adolescent who can perform at a higher level than expected for his or her age. "Creative" suggests that a person can produce new, novel, or different ideas. "Talent" implies a particular area of giftedness, such as artistic talent or mathematical talent.

Ability, intelligence, and aptitude are three closely related concepts. "Ability" encompasses all of the basic cognitive and psychomotor capacities that allow students to learn. "Intelligence" refers chiefly to one class of abilities—cognitive capacities (the ability to think well, solve problems, and use logic). Like talent, "aptitude" denotes relatively specific abilities. For example, the *Differential Aptitude Tests* measure aptitude for numerical reasoning, mechanical reasoning, verbal reasoning, abstract reasoning, space relations, and language usage.

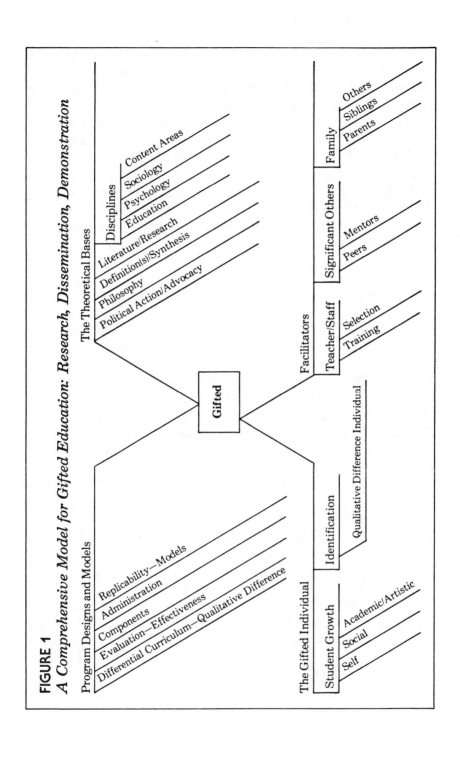

FIGURE 1
A Comprehensive Model for Gifted Education: Research, Dissemination, Demonstration

Four other terms that are widely used in the field of gifted education refer to operations or processes carried out by school personnel: *acceleration, enrichment, screening* and *identification.* Acceleration and enrichment are often antithetical. "Acceleration" describes educational efforts that expose a student either to higher levels or to faster paced instruction than is normal for his or her grade level, while "enrichment" means incorporating additional material or activities into an existing curriculum. "Screening" refers to the preliminary testing and searching to find gifted youth. "Identification" usually denotes the final steps of selecting youngsters who have a need for gifted program services.

The Literature

Certain research and theoretical literature in the field of gifted education provides the base for theoretical and conceptual development of practices in the field. The literature begins with Galton's *Hereditary Genius,* published in 1869, and extends to a great outpouring of new work in the 1970s and early 1980s. New textbooks typically summarize a large part of this literature, and two bibliographic sources specifically provide guides to it. Laubenfels' *The Gifted Student: An Annotated Bibliography* (1977) contains 1,329 annotated references to books and articles. A more recent publication, *The Gifted and Talented, A Bibliography and Resource Guide* (Anthony & Anthony, 1981) provides over 3,000 references, but without annotation.

Conceptual sources for the field of gifted education derive from Renzulli's (1978) work on a definition of giftedness and his instructional model, Stanley's (1980) work on identification through off-grade testing and his work on radical academic acceleration, the work of Maker (1982), VanTassel-Baska (1981), and Kaplan (1974) on curriculum development, Gallagher's (1975) work focusing on academic subject matters, and Treffinger's (1978) and Renzulli's (1979) individualized educational programs for the gifted.

Philosophical Roots

The field of gifted education also has some philosophical bases, which derive from general educational philosophy in the United States. Major tenets of the philosophy are that each individual has a right to an education that fits his or her needs; all individuals should have the opportunity to develop their talents or abilities to the greatest extent; full development of talent in the individual is needed to facilitate self-actualization; our society needs the talented to lead, to solve our problems, and to create/invent a new and better environment; and excellence is the ultimate goal of gifted education.

These philosophical tenets often constitute the unspoken bases of our efforts in gifted education, but all have been discussed, debated, elaborated, and often treated as conflicting or controversial aspects of the field. Of course, the competing philosophy of egalitarianism, calling for equal treatment for all children, is always present.

Political Issues

Gifted education also has been viewed as a political issue and, as such, it has been dealt with at local, state, and federal levels of government as a legislative issue. Federal and state legislation for the gifted was a popular issue in the 1970s. Advocacy groups sprang up at local, state, and national levels to support legislative efforts. Several legislators, including Congressman Carl Pursell and Senator Jacob Javits, led political efforts in support of legislation for gifted education.

Political controversy raged around the organizational structure and location of the Office of the Gifted and Talented in the U.S. Office of Education. Similar battles were fought in many state legislatures. Thus, gifted education has been a political issue during the last decade and probably will continue to be so in the decade of the 1980s.

Too, gifted education is a field that derives its conceptions and structures from several disciplines, particularly education, psychology, development, sociology, and the subject matter disciplines. Therefore, to a great extent the field is interdisciplinary. From psychology, gifted education draws its theoretical bases for identification and theories of learning and motivation. From education, it gets instructional methods. From development, we learn about the normative patterns of cognitive and affective development of the gifted and talented. Sociology offers insights about the behavior of the gifted and their parents in groups. Each of the subject matter disciplines contributes a structure of the knowledge base unique to the discipline along with conceptions of how each field conducts inquiry to arrive at new understanding.

With the realization of all these contributions, future efforts to improve our understanding of the gifted and talented and how to nurture their abilities clearly call for continuing interdisciplinary efforts. And these efforts must be in a cooperative rather than adversarial vein.

THE GIFTED INDIVIDUAL

Giftedness and talent, and the potential for their further development in individuals, are present throughout most of the life cycle. Growth in the areas of one's talent or abilities may be slow or rapid depending upon the conditions of nurturance at home, in school, and in the community. The gifted are not unique individuals; they are simply *qualitatively* different from some other people by virtue of superior potential for development of their talents or abilities. We use scores from tests and rating scales as evidence of that potential, or we may use direct observation of performance or products (inventions, written materials, models) as means of assessing their potential.

Growth is the critical aspect of giftedness. Gifted students should be able to grow more rapidly and to higher levels of achievement than average or low ability students. Growth mainly concerns academic, social, and personal (self) issues.

Academic Growth

Academic growth refers to all the knowledge and skill the student acquires through interaction with school, home, and the world in general. It should come chiefly through school, but for the gifted and talented it often comes through reading and intellectual stimulation with others outside a school setting. The same conditions prevail for youngsters who are artistically talented—growth in artistic skills might come chiefly in a school setting or in experiences outside of school.

Social Growth

Social growth of the gifted and talented is a matter of much concern to parents and teachers because some gifted children have difficulty finding a supportive peer group. Usually children need interaction with peers who share their levels and types of interests and abilities. A gifted child who is enthusiastic about chess, computers, reading, and science may find few or no other children who are interested in or capable of activity in these areas. In that case, the gifted child may seek out older peers or adults or settle for relative isolation.

Special school or community programs for gifted children provide opportunities for appropriate peer interaction. Alternatively, the gifted child often succumbs to the pressure to be "normal" or "average" and gives up his or her interest in advanced topics or activities.

Personal Growth

Self-concept or personality growth in all children involves interaction with other children and perceptual evaluation of those interactions, from which a conception of self emerges. In self-perception there is a need for realism, an understanding of what is perceived, and favorable acceptance of most of the perceived self. Put another way, the individual must be able to accept all elements of self and even find joy or enthusiasm in some elements. If the gifted child enjoys favorable interaction with peers, the emerging self-concept is built upon accurate information about self and enthusiasm about his or her own strong abilities or talents.

Unfortunately, some gifted children encounter hostility from teachers and age peers and have no opportunity to interact with intellectual, academic, or artistic peers. The development of self-concept then faces obstacles. Happily, the rapid growth of school programs for the gifted and talented is providing more and more opportunities for them to have supportive, stimulating interactions with appropriate peers.

Gifted and talented individuals may come to be viewed by teachers and age peers essentially as the embodiment of talent or ability. And programs for the gifted and talented may excessively stress academic or artistic growth. A good program for the gifted and talented concerns itself with *all* aspects of growth.

PROGRAM DESIGNS AND MODELS

During the decade of the 1970s, new program designs and models for the field of gifted education proliferated. Although the pullout program/resource room is the predominant model in gifted programs at the elementary level (Gallagher, Weiss, Oglesby, & Thomas, 1982), it is subject to infinite variation. Many other models have also been developed. Of course, every model has component elements that set it apart from generically similar models. For example, the pullout program in one suburban school district in the Indianapolis area is based on Renzulli's enrichment triad model (1977), but all three stages of activity are done in the pullout program time. In another school, stages one and two are done, as Renzulli advocates, in regular classroom settings. Still other programs vary the goals and activities in a wide variety of ways.

Replicability of model programs is often difficult to achieve because the local descriptive literature does not describe programs in detail unless the program is a dissemination model. The PACE program (Kolloff & Feldhusen, 1981) is a IV-C dissemination model of the program developed by Feldhusen and Kolloff (1978). Joyce Juntune has recently published *Successful Programs for The Gifted and Talented* (1981), which offers detailed descriptions of over 200 elementary, junior high, and high school programs. The descriptions may not be complete enough to permit direct replication, but the programs are all so sufficiently well coded that they permit replication from print materials and on-site visits. Each program likely is strongly characterized by the leaders who developed it or have guided it to the present.

Administration

Administration of these school programs for the gifted and talented often derives authority from the superintendent's office or the school board. The programs are typically managed by a coordinator who has authority only for the program operations. The coordinator must solicit the cooperation of principals and teachers. In larger school systems where the coordinator works with many different buildings, principals, and teachers, the level of cooperation commonly differs substantially from building to building. In some systems individual buildings are permitted to abstain completely from participation in a GT program.

Components

The major components of a GT program may include a planning committee, the coordinator, the identification process, the instructional program services, the teachers, the classroom space, the instructional materials, and the evaluation plan. The components may also include some related services such as guidance and counseling, individual testing, community volunteers and support agencies, and inservice training of teachers. Coordination of all these component activities is typically the responsibility of the local coordinator.

Evaluation

Evaluation of programs is an area of major failure in many GT programs. Typically, little is done other than to solicit attitudinal reactions of children and their parents. Rigorous pretest/posttest assessments of cognitive or affective learning outcomes or comparisons of the GT group performance with a control group of equally able but uninstructed students are rarely carried out.

This failure is evident from a cursory inspection of the sparse evaluation data reported in the program descriptions in Juntune's (1981) book *Successful Programs.* It is also discussed directly by Gallagher et al. (1982) in the report of their survey of GT programs in the United States. Renzulli (1975) has published *A Guidebook for Evaluating Programs for The Gifted and Talented,* an excellent resource to guide evaluation efforts, but it seems to be ignored by most program coordinators. Stevenson and Feldhusen carried out a comprehensive evaluation of a gifted program, which is reported in Stevenson's (1981) thesis. The evaluation could serve as a model for other program evaluators. A minimum level of evaluation of any GT program that has cognitive goals should be pretest/posttest data showing gains or losses of students exposed to the programs.

Curriculum

Program designs for the gifted and talented should be built upon sound curriculum, appropriately differentiated for the special characteristics of the gifted. Maker (1982) has suggested that appropriate curriculum for the gifted must be based on and directed to their special characteristics and needs. Kaplan (1979, p. 5) has also developed a set of "Principles of a Differentiated Curriculum for the Gifted/Talented." Those principles are presented in Figure 2. Although some of the principles would be appropriate to guide curriculum development for average and low ability youth, as a composite they seem to emphasize the higher level operations that should characterize curriculum for the gifted. Virgil Ward had addressed the issue of differentiated curriculum back in 1961 in his book *Differential Education for the Gifted*. Ward particularly emphasized the need for these curricula to be conceptual in nature and to address the major body of conceptual knowledge that is man's heritage.

THE FACILITATORS

The last domain addressed by our comprehensive model is that of the people and agencies that intervene in or interact with the life of the gifted student—hopefully in productive ways.

Parents and Family

Hackney (1981) recently reported some research on the nature of interaction patterns in the families of gifted children. Parents reported that their lifestyles were affected strongly by the presence of a gifted child. Communication between family and school was also an area of great concern to parents. Many parents are hard-pressed to understand the behavior of their gifted children, and few find much help forthcoming from school personnel.

Parents are also deeply concerned that they may fail to nurture the gifted child properly and thereby diminish or destroy the giftedness or talent. And parents are concerned about the relationship of the gifted child with siblings and with other children. New research by Bloom and Sosniak (1981) suggests that the family plays a preeminent role in nurturing the talents of gifted children.

FIGURE 2
Principles of a Differentiated Curriculum for the Gifted/Talented

- Present content that is related to broad-based issues, themes, and problems.
- Integrate multiple disciplines into the area of study.
- Present comprehensive, related, and mutually reinforcing experiences within an area of study.
- Allow for the in-depth learning of a self-selected topic within the area of study.
- Develop independent or self-directed study skills.
- Develop productive, complex, abstract, and higher level thinking skills.
- Focus on open-ended tasks.
- Develop research skills and methods.
- Integrate basic skills and higher level thinking skills into the curriculum.
- Encourage the development of products that challenge existing ideas and produce "new" ideas.
- Encourage the development of products that use new techniques, materials, and forms.
- Encourage the development of self-understanding (i.e., recognizing and using one's abilities, becoming self-directed, appreciating likenesses and differences between oneself and others).
- Evaluate student outcomes by using appropriate and specific criteria through self-appraisal, criterion-referenced, and standardized instruments.

From Sandra N. Kaplan, *Inservice Training Manual: Activities for Developing Curriculum for the Gifted/Talented,* 1979. Printed with permission from the National/State Leadership Training Institute (N/S-LTI-G/T), Office of Superintendent of Ventura County Schools, Ventura, California.

Peers

Other individuals, outside the family, play roles of relative importance in the development and education of gifted and talented children. Peers are a major influence, as noted earlier—but chiefly the intellectual and talented peers. They provide stimulation and interactive feedback that facilitates social and personal development. /

Mentors

Mentors can also be of great importance to the gifted and talented, especially as stimulators and counselors for talent development. The mentor is usually an older person who has some talent, knowledge, or expertise to impart as a model for the gifted or talented student.

Schools

Beyond the family and other individuals, school personnel often have a role in nurturing talent in the gifted. Perhaps the major influence of teachers and counselors comes about when they recognize talent in individual students and provide special assistance, counsel, or guidance to meet the students' individual needs. Much of the school's effort is directed to groups of students. Group efforts may be beneficial to the gifted if students of high ability are grouped together (Kulik & Kulik, 1981), but if the gifted are mixed with children of low and average ability and instruction is group oriented, the gifted may not benefit much.

Teachers of the gifted and talented should be highly able and verbally competent. Above all, they should be proficient in whatever subject matter they are teaching. Recent evidence points to a decline in academic ability among new teachers (Vance & Schlechty, 1982). Thus, gifted students may have fewer competent teachers to serve their needs in the decade ahead.

Selecting and training teachers to serve the gifted and talented deserves careful attention. With the comparatively low salaries paid to teachers now, selection may be limited to those who were not qualified for the more demanding fields. Training rarely begins in undergraduate programs, but many colleges and universities now offer courses, programs, and graduate degrees in education of the gifted and talented. Several states also have laws that provide for certification of teachers to work with the gifted. Thus, a major upgrading may be in progress, and this could eventually yield a substantial number of competent teachers to work with the gifted and talented.

Inservice training of teachers to work with the gifted and talented has spread to thousands of schools in the United States. This type of program can provide valuable upgrading of teachers to work with the gifted and talented. Typical forms of this inservice training include one- to three-day workshops, special classes at conferences, and non-credit educational programs at colleges and universities.

SUMMARY

We have reviewed the comprehensive model for gifted education presented in Figure 1, a constant cycle of research, demonstration and dissemination activities to bring about ever better programs and program components. Unfortunately, little research has been done to provide insights for new program development or to test the effects of programs on gifted students. Even fewer efforts have been directed at building programs from theoretical evidence derived from other fields.

Thus, most extant program models are products of the popular biases or views. These biases include emphases on creativity, problem solving, logic, the Bloom *Taxonomy* (1956), Guilford's *Structure of the Intellect* (1967), independent study, and so on. The only major project with strong empirical validation is the work at Johns Hopkins University.

REFERENCES

Anthony, J.B., & Anthony, M.M. *The gifted and talented, a bibliography and resource guide.* Pittsfield, MA: Berkshire Community Press, 1981.

Bloom, B.S. (Ed.). *Taxonomy of educational objectives. Handbook I: Cognitive domain.* New York: David McKay, 1956.

Bloom, B.S., & Sosniak, L. Talent development versus schooling. *Educational Leadership,* 1981, *39,* 86-94.

Feldhusen, J.F., & Kolloff, M.S. A three-stage model for gifted education. *G/C/T,* 1978, *1,* 3-5, 53-58.

Gallagher, J.J. *Teaching the gifted child.* Boston: Allyn & Bacon, 1975.

Gallagher, J.J., Weiss, P., Oglesby, K., & Thomas, T. *Report on education of gifted I: Surveys of education of gifted students.* Chapel Hill: University of North Carolina, 1982.

Galton, F. *Hereditary genius.* New York: D. Appleton & Co., 1869.

Guilford, J.P. *The nature of human intelligence.* New York: McGraw-Hill, 1967.

Hackney, H. The gifted child, the family, and the school. *Gifted Child Quarterly,* 1981, *25*(2), 51-54.

Juntune, J. *Successful programs for the gifted and talented.* St. Paul, MN: National Association for Gifted Children, 1981.

Kaplan, S.N. *Providing programs for the gifted and talented.* Los Angeles: Leadership Training Institute, 1974.

Kaplan, S.N. *Inservice training manual: Activities for developing curriculum for the gifted/talented.* Los Angeles: Leadership Training Institute, 1979.

Kolloff, M.B., & Feldhusen, J.F. PACE: An application of the Purdue three-stage model. *G/C/T,* 1981, *18,* 47-50.

Kulik, C.L., & Kulik, J.A. Effects of ability grouping on secondary students: A meta-analysis of evaluation findings. *American Educational Research Journal,* 1982, *19,* 415-428.

Laubenfels, J. *The gifted student: An annotated bibliography.* Westport, CT: Greenwood Press, 1977.

Maker, C.J. *Curriculum development for the gifted.* Rockville, MD: Aspen Systems, 1982.

Renzulli, J.S. *A guidebook for evaluating programs for the gifted and talented.* Los Angeles: Leadership Training Institute, 1975.

Renzulli, J.S. *The enrichment triad model.* Mansfield Center, CT: Creative Learning Press, 1977.

Renzulli, J.S. What makes giftedness? *Phi Delta Kappan,* 1978, *60,* 180-184, 261.

Renzulli, J.S. *A guidebook for developing individualized educational programs for gifted and talented students.* Mansfield Center, CT: Creative Learning Press, 1979.

Stanley, J.C. On educating the gifted. *Educational Researcher,* 1980, *9,* 8-12.

Stevenson, D.L. *An evaluation of Project Stretch: A gifted program.* Unpublished master's thesis, Purdue University, 1981.

Treffinger, D.J. Guidelines for encouraging independence and self direction among gifted students. *Journal of Creative Behavior,* 1978, *12,* 14-20.

Vance, V.S., & Schlechty, P.C. The distribution of academic ability in the teaching force: Policy implications. *Phi Delta Kappan,* 1982, *64,* 22-27.

VanTassel-Baska, J. *An administrator's guide to the education of gifted and talented children.* Washington, DC: National Association of State Boards of Education, 1981.

Ward, V.S. *Differential education for the gifted.* Columbus, OH: Charles E. Merrill Publishing Co., 1961.

Instruction for the Gifted: Philosophies and Approaches

Grayson H. Wheatley

Educational programs designed for the gifted will reflect the writer's assumptions about the nature of the learner. Regardless of whether the assumptions are explicitly identified, they determine the curriculum and the instructional methods. The process of identifying one's pedagogical assumptions is a valuable step in preparing or selecting educational materials for gifted students.

PEDAGOGICAL ASSUMPTIONS AND VIEWS

Two contrasting sets of assumptions will be examined. The first set stems largely from *behaviorism*, and the latter reflects a *cognitive* point of view. The writer suggests that, for the gifted, the cognitive position is a more appropriate base for building curriculum.

The Behavioristic View

Much of the current school practice, as determined by textbooks, reflects a behavioristic set of assumptions. In these materials, learning is seen as the process of making associations. These associations are strengthened through repetition with prompt reinforcement of correct responses. The learner is assumed to be, in the John Locke tradition, a *tabula rasa*. The learner assimilates new knowledge in a hierarchical fashion. Thus, it is argued, the content should be broken into small units and carefully sequenced for the learner, with behavioral objectives clearly stated for each unit.

Learning is a process of building up, of putting the small pieces together like building blocks. Learning is the slow accumulation of knowledge through repetitive performance of tasks with selective reinforcement. The sequence of ideas should be fixed by the teacher or curriculum planners. As Gagné (1977) has asserted, any concept or skill can be learned if the individual has the prerequisites.

In accordance with this behavioristic model, curriculum designers are urged to construct learning hierarchies and to check for knowledge of prerequisites. A focus in instructional planning is on sequencing and, most important, reinforcing correct responses so that the proper stimulus-response can be established. This approach results in overemphasis on low-level skills at the expense of principles and strategies. An educational program for the gifted based on these assumptions raises serious questions.

What Is the Nature of Present School Learning?

Primarily because of behavioristic influences, school learning is rule-oriented. Based on analysis of pupil classroom behavior, Eisner (1980) found that pupils are applying rules or memorizing facts most of the time. In school, most tasks are to be performed by applying a rule. Further, students develop a mind-set toward rule applications; they expect to apply a rule rather than exercise reasoning requiring analysis, synthesis, or creativity.

Rule-oriented learning is not to be confused with rule application. Rules are critically important in most, if not all, disciplines. We cannot operate efficiently without a large number of acquired rules. The problem arises when learning becomes rule-oriented, *dominated* by rules. Outside of school, many tasks require original thought and problem solving, in which ideas must be restructured and synthesized.

The rule orientation can be seen by examining current textbooks. Textbooks have indeed changed somewhat over the past 100 years. For example, more use is made of colorful art in textbook design, and the ideas to be learned have become more explicit, even to stating what the learner should know after completing each lesson. But, fundamentally, the emphasis is still on low-level cognitive tasks, especially on learning sets of rules. Rarely are students encouraged to go beyond the data, to solve realistic problems, or build a coherent argument.

Although applying a rule is an appropriate strategy for many tasks, it should not be the only way pupils approach problems. The rule strategy has inherent limitations. A rule will not always suffice; at times decisions must be made.

Schools are rule-oriented for many interrelated, complex reasons. First, low-level cognitive tasks are the easiest to teach and assess. Thus, busy teachers tend to emphasize such tasks. Second, completing a long, detailed assignment exactly as specified (and on time) is thought to somehow build character. This belief has deep philosophic roots extending back to Aristotle. Third, although publishers claim to "give teachers what they want," there is a mind-set in publishing for rule-oriented texts; publishers know how to produce these products and are reluctant to risk a different approach. Fourth, for the past 60 years American education has been dominated by behaviorism, with its emphasis on product rather than process. In mathematics this has meant emphasis on number facts and computational skills. In English it has meant emphasis on grammatical rules and spelling. In social studies it has meant emphasis on names, dates, and places.

The behavioristic approach has been reflected in every discipline of the school curriculum. Though much has been written about teaching for meaning and getting students to think, textbooks still emphasize lower level objectives.

What Are the Outcomes of Rule-Oriented Learning?

When students consistently experience rule-oriented instruction, they come to expect to apply rules and may not develop facility with higher level thought. Whether it is learning facts, definitions, or skills, students come to see learning as following directions. To develop effective patterns of reasoning when required to perform tasks by applying rules most of the time is almost impossible. The "successful" students in our schools are often the ones who abandon thinking and focus on memorizing the patterns of behavior being reinforced by rule-oriented teachers. The end result is a population of students who appear unable to reason. The National Assessment results (Lindquist, Carpenter, Silver, & Matthews, 1983) revealed that American children were quite weak in problem solving.

The Cognitive Approach

In contrast to the behavioristic approach, the cognitive approach (Anderson, 1980; Neisser, 1967; Wittrock, 1979) sees the learner as actively seeking to organize information meaningfully. It is assumed, as Piaget (Piaget & Inhelder, 1969) has demonstrated, that children are constantly reacting to and interpreting environmental stimuli; learners are active rather than passive.

Children naturally try to understand new stimuli. From the moment a child enters this world, he or she is attempting to make sense of all experiences. Rather than being programmed by teachers, children are preprogrammed to learn. According to the cognitivists, children learn best when the learning environment is structured so that they can construct meaning for themselves (Papert, 1980; Wittrock, 1977).

Children construct knowledge for themselves by forming mental representations of interrelated concepts (Neisser, 1967; Skemp, 1979). Bransford and Johnson (1973) have argued that intelligibility requires the construction of representations of what a passage or theory is saying. Skemp (1979) calls these representations *schemas*. Schemas are idiosyncratic and cannot be laid out by an instructor. When information is represented mentally in schemas, new ideas can be related to what is already known. The process of *accommodation* is the revising and extending of existing schemas to explain new knowledge and relating this new knowledge to what is already known. Schemas are multidimensional, elaborate, and dynamic. Furthermore, schemas themselves are organized into higher ordered schemas.

Based on this model, the goal of instruction is to provide a rich environment so that individuals can build their schemas. As Kozmetsky (1980) stated, "Each student must...be encouraged to build his/her own conceptual constructs that will permit the ordering of knowledge into useful problem solving schema" (p. 152). Thus, the teacher's role is to provide stimulating, motivational experiences and act as a guide to children as they build schemas.

In designing these experiences, attention should be focused on guiding the learner in establishing a knowledge framework that will facilitate the understanding of new concepts and principles. Rather than designing a rigid learning environment with highly sequenced steps, the teacher should work to build a stimulating environment that will allow students to construct knowledge for themselves. Often, this means destroying cognitive equilibrium by introducing a discrepant event that will lead to a restructuring of schemas and greater understanding.

As an example, consider the learning of computer programming. Computer programming requires knowledge of a computer language. This means learning the syntax of many computer commands. Typically, it is assumed that students must first memorize the commands and the particular sequence of symbols for using those commands in programming. An alternative approach (Hersberger & Wheatley, 1980) begins with a problem to be solved. The computer commands are then learned in the process of solving the problem. In this way, children can relate what they learn to other ideas (build schemas). Furthermore, by writing programs, they learn the commands when needed rather than in some prescribed order determined by the instructor. Children may learn the commands in a different order—as they need them in their particular problem.

The computer is a particularly appropriate tool for gifted children to learn cognitively in that the child can control the computer. In controlling the computer, the child is free to test hypotheses and determine the order of topics to be investigated.

Finally, the cognitivist assumes that learning is *goal-oriented*. And goals are best set by the individual. At the computer, children can, within reason, explore ideas in an order they set for themselves.

Attention to individual *learning styles* is also important in planning instruction for the gifted. Persons with a *global* learning style (Kagan, Moss, & Sigel, 1963) may profit more from instruction that stresses *figurally* presented information, while persons with an *analytic* learning style may profit more from a dominantly *verbal-symbolic* presentation.

Given the contrasting positions of the behaviorists and the cognitivists, the cognitivist approach clearly seems more appropriate as a psychological basis for designing gifted education curricula. Gifted children are cognitively active and will thus profit greatly from instruction that encourages them to react and organize information for themselves.

INSTRUCTIONAL METHODS

Many instructional models have been developed for educating our youth. This section discusses several approaches that are compatible with cognitive ideas. Instructional methods for the gifted should, first and foremost, provide opportunities for the students to organize their ideas in ways meaningful to them. This suggests that highly structured methods may not be as effective as methods that have built in flexibility. Yet, we recognize that a variety of instructional methods is appropriate. Certain methods may be effective for developing skills, while another method may be more effective for higher level thought. Variety in instructional methods has been shown to be crucially important. /

Cognitive Experience (Piaget/Dewey)

The goal of instruction for the gifted should be to develop original, creative thinkers with a grasp of the fundamental principles in the discipline. Some time should be devoted to acquisition of knowledge, but this must be done in a manner that allows individuals to structure knowledge for themselves. Piaget's constructs of *assimilation* and *accommodation* describe the process well. This method could be viewed as a variation of Dewey's approach, with experience interpreted more as cognitive experience than social/physical experience (Dewey, 1938).

Ward (1961) has suggested that "instruction of intellectually superior individuals should emphasize the central function of meaning in the acquisition of fact and principle..." (p. 161). He further argued that concepts having maximum meaning should be sought for their greater educational value. Ward stressed the importance of learning methods of acquiring knowledge rather than just amassing knowledge.

Discovery Method

The discovery method (Bruner, 1960, 1963) is a highly appropriate instructional mode for the gifted. Through *guided discovery,* the gifted can be led to build knowledge in a meaningful way. The student learns that thinking, reasoning, and questioning are important. Presenting information in a didactic way may on occasion be appropriate, but every effort should be made to structure the learning environment so gifted children can react and interact and build their own mental representations. The *class discussion*, with emphasis on high-level thought, is a variation of the discovery approach. A skillful teacher can lead pupils to think deeply and form their own ideas.

Group Work and Individual Projects

Other methods appropriate for the gifted are small group work and individual projects. Small group discussions allow students to become more aware of their ideas and thought processes (Bloom & Broder, 1963; Whimbey, 1980). Members of the small group can be given a problem to solve and encouraged to work together in reaching a solution. Individual and small group projects are excellent ways to stimulate gifted students to develop their intellect and acquire knowledge in a meaningful way. These techniques can be used effectively in all subjects..

The Feldhusen three-stage model (Feldhusen & Kolloff, 1978) describes a plan for leading gifted students to work independently by beginning with a structured approach. Whatever instructional plans are used, a variety of grouping arrangements, together with independent study, should be utilized.

Advance Organizers

Facts, concepts, and principles should be learned in ways that allow students to be maximally interrelated. This can be achieved by considering a broad conceptualization of ideas that allow the ideas to be understood in context. Providing advance organizers (Ausubel, 1960) is one way to encourage students to focus on meaning.

Facts and Skills

Although this chapter has emphasized higher level thought and problem solving in a curriculum for the gifted, facts and skills must not be neglected. Creative thought is possible only if the individual has the requisite knowledge and skills (Ghiselin, 1952). Teachers should impress upon students the necessity for mastering skills and techniques.

The main issue in this chapter is deciding how this is to be accomplished. At first it may seem logical to insist on mastery of facts and skills before developing the relationships and applications. This approach, however, has serious weaknesses.

First, teachers have difficulty limiting the time devoted to skills development to allow adequate time for higher level thought. Skills training appears to expand to fill the instructional time available. And Skemp (1979) has identified another problem associated with heavy emphasis on facts and skills in isolation: "When particular plans are over-practiced, their connections with their integrating schema may weaken past recall. The advantage of routinizing may then be outweighed by lack of adaptability, since all that is left is a set of fixed habits" (p. 173).

Second, children often are not highly motivated to do the arduous work to achieve mastery of skills. Bright children, particularly, want to understand, to see the big picture. Gifted and talented students may be unwilling to postpone higher level thought.

Given that skills are important, the question is how to organize instruction to achieve the goal of skills development. From a cognitive point of view, facts and skills can be more efficiently and meaningfully acquired within the context of goal-oriented learning. If instruction is organized around a general theme (is goal-oriented), the associated facts and skills can be learned efficiently with less time needed for drill and practice. Skemp (1979) has made the following point:

> When the tasks to be learned fall into a small number of classes, sufficiently alike within each class for the same plan rule to serve, instrumental learning is quicker than learning a schema. ... Paradoxically, in a schema there is more to learn but less to remember—more to learn because higher-order concepts are involved, and more connections, but less to remember because once learned, it forms a cohesive whole, from which an indefinitely large number of particular plans can be derived. (p. 261)

A Problem Solving Approach

In guiding gifted students to learn a particular domain of knowledge, or better still, a method of reasoning, it is useful to begin with a problem. A problem exists in the form of a puzzling phenomenon, an unexplained relationship, or a task without a specific procedure. It is helpful to think of problem solving as what you do when you don't know what to do. The problem solving approach contrasts sharply with rule-oriented learning. Rather than knowing there is a "right way" and seeing the task as remembering the facts and rules that should be used, the learner can reason freely and openly, utilizing any desired methods to understand the problem and find a solution.

Problem solving conditions are created by carefully constructing questions about interesting issues, discrepant events, an experiment, or any variety of puzzling situations. A problem can create a healthy state of disequilibrium. As noted previously, people have a basic drive to make sense out of experience—to reduce cognitive dissonance (Festinger, 1957). When a person is faced with inexplicable events, there is attention and motivation for thought.

Teachers can create situations in which either an apparent contradiction or unexplained phenomenon is present. Teaching in this manner could be called teaching *through* problem solving. Additionally, teaching *about* problem solving is important. Attention to general problem solving heuristics has proven effective (Schoenfeld, 1979; Wheatley & Wheatley, 1982).

In mathematics and science this could take the form of teaching a set of problem solving heuristics. For example:

Guess and test

Look for a pattern

Work backward

Solve a related problem

Draw a diagram

Write an equation.

In English it might be the interpretation of a rich literature passage (What does the author mean?). In social studies it might be interpreting a historical event (e.g., Why was the Panama Canal built?). In science it might be trying to explain an observed phenomenon (e.g., Why did the candle go out?). In mathematics it could be a puzzle or a non-routine word problem.

Also consider the teaching of computer programming. Logically, programming commands should first be learned, and only then applied in solving problems. But commands such as IN-PUT, GOTO, FOR-NEXT, and READ-DATA are meaningless terms until one understands the need for them. Using a problem solving approach, a problem could initially be presented. The teacher could then, through questioning, guide students in developing a sequence of steps for instructing the computer to solve the problem. As the need for a new command arises, the teacher could introduce the word and syntax in context. In this way the students can relate the new information to other knowledge and build a framework (schema) for computer commands. Information learned in context is better remembered and available in the future when needed (Wittrock, 1974).

Whatever the subject—English, social studies, science, mathematics—some will argue that students must first master facts and skills. Although students clearly need facts and skills, the question is whether they should learn them *first.* Wittrock's (1974) generative process of learning suggests that information can be learned and remembered most efficiently through problem solving.

Wheatley (1982) developed an elementary school mathematics program based on problem solving in which one-fourth of the school year was spent on problem solving. A group of 850 fifth-grade pupils showed increases in national percentiles on the *Iowa Test of Basic Skills* from the 40th to the 70th percentile. Although students spent less time on computation, their computation score increases paralleled their application scores. Thus, skills were learned more efficiently when meaningful units were integrated into the curriculum. In contrast, a rule-oriented curriculum discourages the development of higher level thought.

SUMMARY

As students participate in a gifted education program, they come to see learning as an exciting lifelong adventure. Learning can be thought of as a trip on a river of reason. Traveling down a river can be a rich, fulfilling experience, with much satisfaction. Navigating a boat down a river calls for many decisions and frequent problem solving. Even if the navigator has a map, challenging situations will arise because the river is not static, but ever changing.

The River of Reason is a process-oriented river with a strong current of problem solving. And many islands of facts, skills, and rules must be visited to pick up supplies. Although we want to be on the River of Reason most of the time, we must frequently stop at the islands and acquire necessary information and skills.

This perception of learning as a River of Reason is in strong contrast to the Road of Rules. Too frequently, school learning is perceived as a Road of Rules. Students are led down the Road of Rules by a guide who makes the major decisions and insists on close adherence to the rules of the road. The guide makes every effort to choose interesting routes with attractive scenery. But often the traveler is too busy looking at the rule book to enjoy the attractions. Occasionally a traveler becomes lost or decides to take a side trip—usually risking the displeasure of the guide. On these excursions, the traveler may explore exciting new lands, perhaps even ascending a high mountain from which he or she obtains a global perspective. The traveler may even form a mental map of the country, which reduces dependence on the book of rules.

We are in an era when reasoning and problem solving are becoming increasingly important. In the marketplace, jobs requiring repetitive operations with little cognitive demand are diminishing rapidly as a result of automation. The world faces enormous problems, which call for creative thinking. The gifted in our schools represent the pool from which the leaders of tomorrow are likely to come. We must have a curriculum that allows these individuals to develop their potential for original thought.

REFERENCES

Anderson, J.R. *Cognitive psychology and its implications.* San Francisco: Freeman, 1980.

Ausubel, D. The use of advanced organizers in the learning and retention of meaningful verbal material. *Journal of Educational Psychology,* 1960, *51,* 267-272.

Bloom, B., & Broder, L. *Problem-solving processes of college students.* Chicago: University of Chicago Press, 1963.

Bransford, J., & Johnson, M. Consideration of some problems of comprehension. In W. Chase (Ed.), *Visual information processing: Proceedings.* New York: Academic Press, 1973.

Bruner, J. *The process of education.* Cambridge, MA: Harvard University Press, 1960.

Bruner, J. *On knowing.* Cambridge, MA: Harvard University Press, 1963.

Dewey, J. *Experience and education.* New York: Macmillan, 1938.

Eisner, E. Future priorities for curriculum reform. *Educational Leadership,* 1980, *37*(6), 453-456.

Feldhusen, J., & Kolloff, M. A three-stage model for gifted education. *G/C/T,* 1978, *1,* 3-5, 53-58.

Festinger, L. *A theory of cognitive dissonance.* Evanston, IL: Row Peterson, 1957.

Gagné, R. *Conditions of learning* (3rd ed.). New York: Holt, Rinehart & Winston, 1977.

Ghiselin, B. *The creative process.* New York: New American Library, 1952.

Hersberger, J., & Wheatley, G. A proposed model for a gifted elementary school mathematics program. *Gifted Child Quarterly,* 1980, *24*(1), 37-40.

Kagan, J., Moss, H., & Sigel, I. Psychological significance of styles of conceptualizations. In J. Wright & J. Kagan (Eds.), Basic cognitive process in children. *Monographs of the Society for Research in Child Development,* 1963, *28,* 73-112.

Kozmetsky, G. The significant role of problem solving in education. In O. Tuma & F. Reif (Eds.), *Problem solving and education: Issues in teaching and research.* Hillsdale, NJ: Lawrence Erlbaum Assoc., 1980.

Lindquist, M.L., Carpenter, T.P., Silver, E.A. & Matthews, W. The third national mathematics assessment: Results and implications for elementary and middle schools. *Arithmetic Teacher,* 1983, *31*(4), 14-19.

Neisser, U. *Cognitive psychology.* New York: Appleton-Century-Crofts, 1967.

Papert, S. *Mindstorms.* New York: Basic Books, 1980.

Piaget, J., & Inhelder, B. *The psychology of the child.* New York: Basic Books, 1969.

Schoenfeld, A. Explicit heuristic training as a variable in problem solving. *Journal for Research in Mathematics Education,* 1979, *10,* 173-187.

Skemp, R. *Intelligence, learning, and action.* New York: John Wiley & Sons, 1979.

Ward, V. *Educating the gifted: An axiomatic approach.* Columbus, OH: Charles E. Merrill, 1961.

Wheatley, G. *A problem solving approach to elementary school mathematics.* Unpublished manuscript, Purdue University, 1982.

Wheatley, G., & Wheatley, C. *Calculator use and problem solving strategies of sixth grade pupils* (Final report). West Lafayette, IN: National Science Foundation, 1982.

Whimbey, A. Students can learn to be better problem solvers. *Educational Leadership,* 1980, *37*(7), 560-563.

Wittrock, M. Learning as a generative process. *Educational Psychologist,* 1974, *11,* 87-95.

Wittrock, M. *The human brain.* Englewood Cliffs, NJ: Prentice-Hall, 1977.

Wittrock, M. The cognitive movement in instruction. *Educational Research,* 1979, *8,* 5-11.

Appropriate Curriculum for the Gifted

Joyce VanTassel-Baska

Perhaps one of the biggest challenges facing gifted education today is the concern of appropriate curriculum. Should curriculum for the gifted be viewed as a separate area of endeavor, an adaptation of good general curriculum practices, or a division of special educational practices? Are good teaching techniques and good teaching methodology all that gifted children need, indicating modification of the instructional pattern but not the

45

curriculum? Should curriculum for the gifted be predetermined and stated on paper or be viewed as a set of experiences inherently to be organized by the child and brought out through interest assessments and appropriate teacher facilitation? Are individualized education programs (IEPs) the answer for gifted children? Or is there more to be considered in providing an appropriate curriculum for this group of children?

A BRIEF HISTORICAL BACKGROUND

The field of gifted education throughout most of its history has been concerned with the phenomenon of giftedness rather than the nurturance of that phenomenon. Terman (1921– 1959) provided the foundational basis for at least three important aspects of gifted education: (1) the differential characteristics found in gifted children, (2) the research base to dispel common myths about the gifted, and (3) a specific tool for identifying intellectually gifted children, the *Stanford-Binet Intelligence Scale.*

Follow-up work by Hollingworth (1942) focused on testing and carrying out additional research on the highly gifted child. She also offered special classes in New York City to such youngsters. Guilford (1956) further advanced knowledge about the phenomenon of giftedness by examining a cellular approach to intelligence, factoring approximately 120 different kinds of ability, which led the way to a broader concept of giftedness as evidenced by the current federal definition (Public Law 95-560):

> The term "Gifted and Talented Children" means children and, whenever applicable, youth, who are identified at the preschool, elementary, or secondary level as possessing demonstrated or potential abilities that give evidence of high performance capability in areas such as intellectual, creative, specific academic, or leadership ability, or in the performing and visual arts, and who by reason thereof, require services or activities not ordinarily provided by the school.

Research into appropriate curriculum for gifted children is much more recent. Until the Sputnik era of the late 1950s—which resulted in programs that addressed specific content areas—few ideas about differentiated curriculum for the gifted had been systematically studied. Even though special classes had been in operation since 1919 in selected locations such as New York and Cleveland, the actual differences in instructional strategies, content, or materials were not examined. Grouping based on intelligence and achievement was the predominant strategy employed, and curriculum outlines and sometimes units were prepared for use with the identified gifted students (Hollingworth, 1926; Hall, 1956).

Over the last 20 years, however, educators in the field of the gifted have conceptualized some general principles about appropriate curriculum for gifted children. Ward (1961) developed a theory of differential education for the gifted that established specific principles around which an appropriate curriculum for the gifted could be developed. Meeker (1969) used the Guilford structure of intellect (SOI) to arrive at student profiles highlighting areas of strength and weakness so that curriculum planners could build a gifted program to improve weak areas. Curriculum workbooks were structured specifically to address this need in the areas of memory, cognition, convergent thinking, divergent thinking, and evaluation. Renzulli (1975) focused on a differentiated curriculum model that moved the gifted child from enrichment exposure activities through training in thinking and research skills into a project-oriented program that dwelt on real problems to be solved. Gallagher (1975) stressed content modification in the core subject areas of language arts, social studies, mathematics, and science. Stanley, Keating, and Fox (1974) concentrated on a content acceleration model to differentiate programs for the gifted.

Recent writings, including Feldhusen and Kolloff (1978), Kaplan (1979), and Maker (1982), have stressed a confluent approach to differentiation of curriculum for the gifted that includes both acceleration and enrichment strategies. Passow and his colleagues (1982) have formulated seven cardinal curriculum principles that reflect content, process, product, behavioral and evaluative considerations.

STATE OF THE ART

In examining the state of the art with respect to curriculum, one is struck by the abstract broadness of the principles compared to the one-dimensionality of the practice. To implement appropriate curriculum for gifted students, there must be concern for the translation of theoretical principles into good practice in a holistic manner rather than piecemeal so that education of the gifted is complete and not fragmented. This can be accomplished if we focus on the core elements to be addressed:

1. Gifted children learn at a different rate from other groups of children, and accommodating that rate is crucial to their development (Keating, 1976). Further, differences in rate or pace can be so great that these necessitate differences in *kind*, not merely degree, of instruction (Ward, 1961).

2. Gifted children crave *depth* in key areas of learning. Educators have addressed this need through "enrichment," which tends to become a superficial add-on to the curriculum. The issue of depth in terms of gifted children cannot be addressed by this type of approach.

   It can be addressed by examining key areas of learning in terms of their essence, their core, their inherent concepts, and exploring with gifted children through Socratic means what these key concepts are and how they relate to all areas of learning. Appropriate learning materials for such work include *Civilization* by Kenneth Clark (1969), *Ascent of Man* by Jacob Bronowski (1973), and *Connections* by James Burke (1978).

3. Gifted children need the challenge and stimulation of being together for at least part of every school day, with expectation levels set high enough to stretch their

potential ability to realize them. Further, setting high expectation levels does not imply more work at low levels of difficulty, but, rather, unending work at complex levels of operation. In that sense, meaningful work for the gifted is that which creates more questions that need exploration and lead to continued study on an individual or small group basis. These expectations can be set and worked on only in a climate in which children have similar levels of ability and understanding. Therefore, grouping of gifted children becomes essential.

4. Gifted children need programs and services across the span of years that they are in school. Their giftedness frequently manifests itself by age 3 and requires nurturance on a regular basis from that time forward. Thus, K–12 articulated planning and programming for all gifted students is essential.

Once these elements have been internalized about the "aura" of the curriculum, we can begin to examine the areas of content learning that are most facilitative for gifted students.

TRADITIONAL CONTENT LEARNING

The myth persists that some semblance of a program is better than no program at all. Once students are in a gifted program, they tend to respond favorably to it, regardless of either its structure or its focus. Consequently, we in this field are sometimes hard pressed to show that the *nature* of a particular treatment has made a difference, as opposed to the mere fact that some treatment occurred. Even positive evaluations overall may be more a manifestation of the Hawthorne effect* than "significant difference." Many gifted programs, just by their existence, offer emotional and motivational support for many gifted children, who then "take off" on their own.

*The Hawthorne effect refers to the positive effect brought about by the act of experimentation itself, based on a set of studies and conducted at the Hawthorne plant of the Western Electric company by researcher Elton Mayo from 1923–1932.

By the same token, as we become more knowledgeable about identifying talent at early ages, we must plan for programmatic intervention much more carefully and consistently. Solid research shows that mathematical talent and foreign language ability can be most economically developed through an accelerative mode (Stanley et al., 1974; Keating, 1976; Van-Tassel-Baska, 1981). Only descriptive studies imply that enrichment is useful to a student's fuller understanding of the world (Gallagher, 1975). We have teachers who are trained to teach content. We may have teachers who can teach creative processes. We know that schools are organized to handle gifted children best within content areas (especially at grades 7–12). Based on these observations, it seems prudent to build a foundational program for gifted students within the basic domains of knowledge—the sciences, mathematics, the humanities, the social sciences, and the behavioral sciences.

Why should curriculum for the gifted be conceptualized within the framework of the basic domains of knowledge? To satisfy gifted students' need for depth, exposure to these traditional areas of learning is essential, not only to develop and refine proficiency skills in verbal and quantitative areas, but also to allow for expanded growth into related disciplines and interdisciplinary studies. A firm understanding of a field of inquiry must precede "creative dabbling." Gifted writers have thoroughly mastered techniques of writing and have refined their skills through repeated practice. The "creative" aspect of writing demands a high level of proficiency in the skill and repeated use of both ends of the writing implement before a product could be perceived as art. By the same token, gifted students benefit greatly from curriculum experiences that go beyond and across the traditional content areas in order to acquire an integrated understanding of knowledge. Curriculum for the gifted should connote the literal meaning of the Latin root for the term "education"—a "leading out" from one point in experience to view the larger perspective.

A curriculum that does not have a strong content base or focus has little richness. And, in reality, identifying aptitude that corresponds to a content area such as mathematics and the verbal arts is far easier than conceptualizing programming in another fashion. Specific content areas provide the appropriate match for specific aptitudes. We would not think of providing a child with high musical aptitude a program in futuristics or an independent study in building an electrical car. Yet, these practices are frequently applied to students who have readily identifiable aptitudes in specific academic areas. Students with high mathematical aptitude should receive a strong program in mathematics concepts and systems.

By this rather obvious connection, we do not intend to imply that serving the gifted appropriately requires only a direct match to a specific identified aptitude area. In the minds of most educators of gifted students, much more is needed. The research base on the positive effects of this approach with precocious students, however, is impressive (Stanley et al., 1974; Durden, 1979). Yet, this deceptively simple approach of matching aptitudes to curriculum offerings rarely occurs in the average elementary school in this country, and is subverted at the middle school and high school levels by inflexible scheduling and programming.

Misconceptions in Teaching Traditional Content

Perhaps traditional content domains have been passed over for curricular work in the education of the gifted because of several misconceptions. One of these is that the gifted "get" these content areas in their regular school program and, therefore, the gifted should have a "special" curriculum. Unfortunately, the content that the gifted receive is minimal compared to what they are capable of learning. If content were rearranged and restructured around a conceptual framework, the gifted could master whole content areas in half the time currently spent.

This compression of content facilitates both proficiency and learning conceptual wholes. It also allows more time for gifted learners to pursue related areas of interest. For example, the gifted can master all the principles of English grammar and syntax in less than four weeks of instruction in any given year. By demonstrating this proficiency on a criterion-referenced test, they then can begin to apply that knowledge to their specific areas of language interest: a course in Latin, a workshop in composition writing, a debate team. Instead, we tend to introduce grammar in minute sections, drag it out over 12 years of English instruction, and never present it so that the gifted have the opportunity to grasp the total linguistic picture or to learn new language systems.

Another misconception is that content acceleration merely means moving through the same material faster. In reality, good content acceleration allows for faster pacing of well-organized, compressed, and appropriate learning experiences for the gifted. Real enrichment for the gifted in the content areas can occur *only* if a fast-paced compressed model is utilized.

A third misconception concerning the use of content areas with gifted students is that there are more important areas of learning for them to explore for purposes of developing their potential creativity. Yet, creativity without subject matter competency has no meaning (Stanley, 1980). Creative mathematicians in real life must be proficient in mathematics before they can apply math principles and concepts in new and diverse ways. Even in applied areas of endeavor such as engineering, medicine, and education, conceptual proficiency in core content domains of knowledge is critical.

Values Education

Most would agree that high-level ability that is not directed in socially constructive ways may be socially dangerous. Thus, curriculum for the gifted should include components of values education through which students can learn to examine their own values, as well as the values of others. Some research tends to suggest that gifted students often are much concerned about the moral and ethical dimensions of questions (Gallagher, 1975). Therefore, the study of competing value systems would serve to enhance the understanding of an area of identified interest. Assuming that gifted students often become the leaders of tomorrow, the moral, social, and ethical dimensions of topics seem particularly relevant as an area for study.

THINKING SKILLS LEARNING

If accelerative and in-depth experiences are provided to the gifted as a framework, the development of skills in critical or creative thinking and research can become an overlay to programs, even though they have been conceptualized in a content modality. By their nature, good critical and creative thinking experiences are adaptable with respect to content, age level, and the experience of participants. These experiences tend to be presented through teaching strategies that create diverse and motivated responses. Their purpose is primarily to provide a prelude to analytical and creative endeavors, regardless of type, and to open up children to fuller expression of their potential (Feldhusen & Kolloff, 1978). Since this is the case, restructuring and infusing a program with these aspects of the curriculum is easier than sacrificing traditional content areas or treating them as an add-on to the curriculum.

Development of process skills in students should be viewed as basic to their curriculum and begun as soon as they enter school. These "basics for the gifted" would reflect practice in the following skill areas:

- —critical thinking
- —creative thinking
- —problem solving
- —research
- —decision making

Each of these skills should be linked directly to a content domain. Thus, gifted students would learn problem solving in mathematics, critical thinking in literature, and decision making in history. Skill development in all five areas is stressed on a hierarchical K–12 basis. This approach appears to be promising in light of the lack of research on process programs that demonstrate transfer of these skills to content dimensions after the skills have been mastered in isolation.

LEARNING THE ARTS

Certainly gifted children need the rigor of a program in a content area in which they excel, coupled with the overlay of the process skills of critical and creative thinking, and research. In addition to these components, gifted children need the arts for development of high intellectual potential, and they need them as early as kindergarten. A good gifted program should incorporate the arts, both in terms of developing performance skills and developing aesthetic judgment throughout the education continuum. For students with special abilities in these areas, intensive training may be most appropriate.

Why the arts? Real enrichment, it can be argued, consists of offering new awareness about the world that has a deep relevance to the individual. Surely the arts can offer this in a way that other fields cannot, for the arts tap into the emotional center of human beings. We are responsive to art and music and the performing arts because we are human, and they touch us as human beings. The immense difference one senses in live performance versus the electronically filtered reproduction of a recording makes the point eloquently.

What we know about the nature of the gifted child would lead us to include a strong component in the arts. Differential characteristics such as high-level sensitivity, keenness of perception, and the ability to understand interrelationships and grasp meanings (Clark, 1980) all reflect a need for exposure to aesthetic experiences that allow for further development of these traits. In addition, research studies on eminence point to the passion for and importance of the arts displayed by individuals who were exceptional in fields other than artistic endeavor (Cox 1926; Goertzels & Goertzels, 1962).

Teaching the arts to the gifted is also particularly critical in developing an understanding of self and others, based on the interrelationship of thoughts and feelings. All of the arts offer a medium for understanding the congruence of ideas and emotions. The arts provide direct access to emotional response, but through a rational process and presentation. The arts can be a vehicle for developing aesthetic judgment, thus offering many opportunities for the acquisition of evaluation skills. Setting criteria to measure the value of art objects, a piece of music, or a performance provides valuable experience for gifted students to act as "critics" and to develop the intellectual framework for this kind of effort.

Offering an arts component in a curriculum for the gifted can be a good stimulus for some students to begin the formal study of a particular area. For example, a student may wish to pursue musicology as a result of early music experiences. Or another may wish to intern in a museum to learn the job of curator. Thus, career exploration can be merged with serious study in a specific area of interest.

The arts also lend themselves well to development of meaningful projects, not only in terms of conceptualization but also in terms of the actual mode of presentation. Children who have experienced theater are more apt to try to create it than those who have not. Similarly, children exposed to the visual arts are more apt to employ them in a creative product. Consequently, product development can be enhanced greatly by systematic work in the arts.

Relating the arts in some manner also offers to gifted children an excellent opportunity to analyze and synthesize information in the aesthetic domain. It builds on their strong ability to grasp interrelationships and comprehend meaning at high levels. Deliberately planned experiences that use "forced association" as a technique work well in the arts and begin to move children toward free association among other arts experiences. At junior high and high school levels, the interrelationships can take the form of a humanities program in which the arts are seen as an avenue to other fields such as philosophy, history, and literature.

ADDITIONAL SERVICES AND PROGRAMS

Traditional content, process skills, and the arts have been strongly argued as key components in an ideal curriculum for the gifted. And other special services and programs uniquely appropriate for this population are needed as well. Areas such as counseling, career education, and mentorships should be considered.

Counseling

Counseling is not usually considered a part of curriculum. Yet, it is a service that provides the key framework for the curriculum delivery system to work for gifted students. Therefore, counseling services become a curricular concern. Particularly at middle school and high school levels, counseling (or lack of it) determines what courses students take and what level of course. For gifted students to receive appropriate curriculum, they must be informed about specific courses that address their area(s) of strength. In addition, gifted students should have the opportunity to understand and cope with their exceptionality in small group sharing sessions, receive training in decision making skills, and be provided alternative choices involving course taking, colleges, and careers (VanTassel-Baska, 1983).

Counseling for the gifted should occur over the span of school years. Although coping skills may be most critical at the elementary level, academic counseling becomes important by junior high school, as decisions often have to be made four years in advance. Choices of what college to attend and what career to pursue become important counseling issues by ninth grade and should be reflected in a specific structured program provided by the school. Parent involvement in all aspects of the counseling program is essential, as is the use of teachers performing the counseling function. Utilization of counseling specialists may be necessary in the case of gifted youths who experience unusual difficulty in adjustment, achievement, and other school-related issues.

Career Education

Concern for career education for gifted individuals stems from their natural profusion of riches in regard to life's alternatives. Because many of these students are good at so many kinds of tasks, to focus attention and energy on one line of endeavor is sometimes difficult and even painful for them. Career education can enhance their powers of decision making by enabling informed choices, based on assessments of strengths, interests, and values (Hoyt & Hebeler, 1974).

By the same token, some gifted students are very sure at an early age about the career avenue they wish to pursue. Career education can supplement these students' avid interest in a field by providing internship experiences in the desired career area as early as junior high school. In addition, it can help both student and parent plan ahead for educational experiences that would be most profitable, given the clarity of choice. And many times irrelevant requirements can be avoided if the course of study is well defined (VanTassel-Baska, 1981).

Mentorships

Much of the research on eminent persons clearly points to the profound influence of a single tutor/friend/family member on the gifted child (Cox, 1926; Goertzels & Goertzels, 1962; Bloom & Sosniak, 1981). Both as an aid to cognitive learning and for emotional support, the one-to-one relationship has provided special benefits for the development of exceptional potential.

Although the tutorial approach may be ideal, it is hardly practical for schools to consider for more than a few students, and rather difficult for parents to implement on their own. But creating the opportunity for gifted children to experience a mentor relationship on a limited basis still can be seen as facilitative to their development.

Creating a mentorship experience requires two fundamental steps: (1) developing a resource bank of adults in the community who have an interest in working with gifted students and who have high-level expertise in a particular area, and (2) identifying students who can profit from exposure to these adults and who share similar abilities and interests with the chosen mentor. A structured mentorship program can focus on a contract between student and mentor for the completion of specific tasks or a project over a predetermined time period. Other collaborative opportunities can develop out of the working relationship that is established, such as an "apprenticeship" situation in a research laboratory, a joint publication, or a shared presentation at a professional meeting.

KEY ISSUES IN DEVELOPMENT AND IMPLEMENTATION OF CURRICULUM

A curriculum for the gifted must be more than the sum of the components just discussed. It must represent an interaction among the content dimension, the instructional dimension, and the logistical dimension. Though the scope of this chapter concerns itself primarily with the content dimension, certain logistical issues that provide the framework and setting for the delivery of content merit comment.

Principles and Instructional/Logistical Implications

The curriculum committee of the Leadership Training Institute (LTI) has conceptualized seven principles that contain both instructional and logistical implications in a curriculum for gifted students (Passow, 1982):

1. The content of curricula for the G/T should focus on and be organized to include more elaborate, complex, and in-depth study of major ideas, problems, and themes that integrate knowledge within and across systems of thought.

2. Curricula for the G/T should allow for the development and application of productive thinking skills to enable students to reconceptualize existing knowledge and/or generate new knowledge.

3. Curricula for the G/T should enable them to explore constantly changing knowledge and information and develop the attitude that knowledge is worth pursuing in an open world.

4. Curricula for the G/T should encourage exposure to, selection of, and use of specialized and appropriate resources.

5. Curricula for the G/T should promote self-initiated and self-directed learning and growth.

6. Curricula for the G/T should provide for the development of self-understanding and the understanding of one's relationship to persons, societal institutions, nature and culture.

7. Evaluations of curricula for the G/T should be conducted in accordance with prior stated principles, stressing higher level thinking skills, creativity, and excellence in performance and products.

In addition to the stated principles, four other issues reflect on the curriculum process: scope and sequence, differentiation, grouping, and articulation.

Scope and Sequence

Good curriculum must reflect progressive development in both skill and content arenas (Tyler, 1958) so that appropriate pacing and diversity are maintained. Student interest should be a prime input factor in modifying curricular units and teacher expectations with regard to the expansion of educational and cultural opportunities for gifted students.

The curriculum should reflect provisions for accelerating skill building in the areas of reading, writing, research, the use of computers and scientific apparatus, and mathematical problem solving. It should demonstrate well-planned sequential development of increasingly difficult content and processes and include materials and activities that will provide for the development of skills in group and individual problem solving and decision making. Interdisciplinary curriculum units should provide for conceptual development over time. Themes such as man's search for identity, the question of authority, and the concept of unity could be explored at several grade levels with more sophisticated objectives in mind at each succeeding level.

The scope of full-time curriculum for the gifted should be broad-based and as comprehensive as possible, given the level of ability and interest of the students. At the same time, curriculum experiences must be carefully structured to promote maximum learning in specific aptitude areas.

Differentiation

Most gifted programs, it is generally agreed, should be distinguished from regular programs by placing *more* emphasis on the following curriculum considerations:

1. *Principle of economy.* This principle seeks to delete or compress a gifted student's basic curriculum in content skills that he or she has mastered independently or can master quickly if the organization of content focuses on concept mastery. Thus, a student who comes to school reading holistically would not be expected to spend kindergarten and first grade in reading readiness programs or heavy phonics training. Rather, a reading program would be devised focusing on developmental reading skills such as vocabulary, comprehension, and interpretation. Phonics work would be organized into a set of skills for quick mastery by this student.

2. *Concentration on higher level thinking skills.* This principle focuses on the development of thinking skills as an important tool for the gifted student in being a producer rather than a consumer of knowledge. Application of skills such as critical and creative thinking are seen as essential for meaningful work in any context.

3. *Concentration on the interrelationships between and among bodies of knowledge.* The need to focus on depth in the curriculum plan developed for the gifted is embodied in this principle. Based on Ward's (1961) theory of differential education for the gifted, it establishes the concept of content integration by schemas and systems for the gifted as the highest order of importance.

4. *Exposure to nontraditional school subjects.* Gifted students should be exposed to challenging areas of traditional liberal arts curriculum not offered in elementary

and secondary schools such as logic, law, and philosophy. Early exposure and training in foreign language at the elementary level could also be seen as an offering in this context.

5. *Self-directed learning.* Gifted students should develop responsibility, taking charge of their own learning and growth. Upon demonstrating such responsibility, more program options of an independent nature can be offered.

6. *Commitment to future learning.* This principle relates to gifted students becoming sensitive to the knowledge explosion and the impact of technology on the task of learning, with the view that learning will be a fulfilling, lifelong pursuit.

Grouping

Most educators who work with the gifted believe that the practice of putting youngsters of similar abilities, interests, and learning styles together for large portions of time is hard to equal. Gifted youngsters enjoy more than almost anything else the opportunity to exchange ideas among themselves without fear of being laughed at or scorned. Some programs group youngsters only periodically, or for a certain period each day. In any case, extensive grouping by interest and ability is needed for gifted students to fully develop their potential.

Full-time grouping facilitates the opportunity for student growth in ways that are not possible under other arrangements (Bent, 1968). And this approach allows a program to reveal effectiveness much more readily. The historical development of gifted programs highlights the strong relationship between the longevity of a program and its grouping patterns. Both the Cleveland Major Work Program and the Bronx High School of Science have survived over 50 years, employing full-time grouping of gifted students in all academic areas. Comprehensive programs for the gifted, then, should utilize full-time grouping strategies to enhance continuity of individual student progress as well as the continuity and effectiveness of the overall program.

FIGURE 3
Essential Curriculum Components for Gifted Students

I. Acceleration of content based on proficiency levels in:
- reading
- math

I. Acceleration of content based on proficiency levels in:
- reading
- math
- science
- social studies
- language arts
- art
- music

I. Access to high school coursework in selected content areas

I. Access to upper level high school and/or college courses

Advanced placement courses according to strength areas

Foreign language instruction—third and fourth year of a foreign language

II. Enrichment examples:
- Problem solving strategies
- Science experimentation via computers
- Expository and creative writing
- Creative dramatics
- Introduction of foreign languages (Latin, French, Spanish)
- Development of critical and creative thinking skills
- Learning of basic research skills on topics of interest

II. Enrichment examples:
- A computer literacy program
- Foreign language instruction
- Research projects
- Theater arts
- Junior Great Books
- Man: A Course of Study (MACOS)
- Art and music appreciation
- Logic

II. Enrichment examples:
- Foreign language instruction second year
- A course in logic
- Selective reading and discussion groups
- Humanities course
- Writing computer programs
- Advanced research projects

II. Enrichment examples:
- Art appreciation
- Music appreciation
- Leadership
- Psychology
- Anthropology
- Urban planning
- Political science
- Law
- Creativity

Program Articulation

Any school district that takes on the task of developing a gifted program must carefully consider an overall articulation plan that allows for identification of its gifted population at the kindergarten level and offers appropriate programming for that population on a K–12 basis. In many districts funds do not exist to implement a total program in any given year, but total articulation can be accomplished within a reasonable span of time. An example might be a three-year plan in which K–3 students and identified high school students receive programming during year one, students in grades 4–6 in year two, and 7–8 in the third year. In this way, all students identified in year one will receive appropriate services from the point of identification, yet the district will have an opportunity to stagger its program implementation.

Program articulation of this kind is important for several reasons:

1. Once a student has been identified and offered a program at any given level, he or she has the right to expect that it will continue on the same basis.
2. Since content acceleration is and should be a facet of many gifted programs, students should not have to return to a level of work below their state of advancement.
3. Growth gains and attitude changes can be adversely affected by programs coming too late in a student's career or stopping in the middle.

AN IDEAL CURRICULUM FOR THE GIFTED

Figure 3 attempts to delineate and apply all the curricular components discussed in this chapter. It highlights the need for content specialization. It attends to the need for acceleration, enrichment, and other special services in educating the gifted. It recognizes the role of thinking skills in developing students' potential, and it provides appropriate experiences in the arts. It demonstrates progressive and sequential development of broad curriculum areas on a K–12 basis and suggests the need for comprehensive services across the span of school years. It highlights differentiation issues in an integrated fashion. We hope it will serve as a guide for schools and parents in making sound educational decisions around curriculum alternatives for gifted and talented students.

Specifically, curriculum can be divided into five sections: acceleration of content, enrichment, counseling, special instruction, and mentor arrangements. The figure provides examples of topics/courses that might be offered at a grade level cluster. Sequence of a topic or content area is suggested across clusters by section. The intent of the figure is to be illustrative of the ideas and principles discussed in this chapter, not prescriptive for any given school program.

SUMMARY

This chapter has advocated a position that views a content-based curriculum as the core of any program for gifted and talented students. It has argued for including traditional subject matter areas taught from a process perspective with experiences in the arts. It has demonstrated that conceptual learning and enrichment in the content areas must be accompanied by appropriate content acceleration allowing for both pacing and depth. It asserts the need for a full-time grouping model to accommodate a full range of comprehensive articulated programs and services to gifted students at all grade levels.

REFERENCES

Bent, L. *An experimental study of grouping the gifted.* Unpublished report, Illinois Office of Education, 1968.

Bloom, B. & Sosniak, L. Talent development versus schooling. *Educational Leadership,* 1981, *39,* 86-94.

Bronowski, J. *Ascent of man.* Boston: Little, Brown, 1973.

Burke, J. *Connections.* Boston: Little, Brown, 1978.

Clark, B. *Growing up gifted.* Columbus, OH: Charles E. Merrill Publishing Co., 1980.

Clark, K. *Civilization.* New York: Harper & Row, 1969.

Cox, C.M. *Genetic studies of genius* (Vol. 2). Stanford, CA: Stanford University Press, 1926.

Durden, W. The Johns Hopkins program for verbally gifted youth. *Roeper Review,* 1979, *2*(3), 34–37.

Feldhusen, J., & Kolloff, M. A three-stage model for gifted education. *G/C/T,* 1978, *1,* 53-58.

Gallagher, J.J. *Teaching the gifted child* (2nd ed.). Boston: Allyn & Bacon, 1975.

Goertzels, V., & Goertzels, M. *Cradles of eminence.* Boston: Little, Brown, 1962.

Guilford, J. The structure of the intellect. *Psychological Bulletin,* 1956, *53,* 267-293.

Hall, T. *Gifted children, the Cleveland story.* Cleveland, OH: World Publishing Co., 1956.

Hollingworth, L. *Gifted children.* New York: World Book Co., 1926.

Hollingworth, L. *Children above 180 I.Q.* New York: World Book Co., 1942.

Hoyt, K., & Hebeler, J. *Career education for the gifted and talented.* Salt Lake City, UT: Olympus Publishing Co., 1974.

Kaplan, S. Language arts and social studies curriculum in the elementary school. In H. Passow (Ed.), *The gifted and talented: Their education and development* (78th yearbook of the National Society for the Study of Education, Part 1). Chicago: University of Chicago Press, 1979.

Keating, D. *Intellectual talent: Research and development.* Baltimore: Johns Hopkins University Press, 1976.

Maker, C.J. *Curriculum development for the gifted.* Rockville, MD: Aspen Systems, 1982.

Meeker, M. *The structure of intellect: Its interpretations and uses.* Columbus, OH: Charles E. Merrill Publishing Co., 1969.

Passow, A.H. *LTI committee report.* Unpublished report, National/ State Leadership Training Institute of the Gifted and Talented, 1982.

Renzulli, J. *The enrichment triad.* Wethersfield, CT: Creative Learning Press, 1975.

Stanley, J. On educating the gifted. *Educational Researcher,* 1980, *9,* 8-12.

Stanley, J., Keating, D., & Fox, L. *Mathematical talent: Discovery, description, and development.* Baltimore: Johns Hopkins University Press, 1974.

Terman, L. (Ed.). *Genetic studies of genius* (5 vols.). Stanford, CA: Stanford University Press, 1921-1959.

Tyler, R. *Principles of curriculum and instruction.* Chicago: University of Chicago Press, 1958.

VanTassel-Baska, J. A comprehensive model of career education for gifted. *Journal of Career Education,* 1981, *7*(4), 325-331.

VanTassel-Baska, J. (Ed.). *A practical guide to the counseling of the gifted in a school setting.* Reston, VA: Council for Exceptional Children, 1983.

Ward, V. *Educating the gifted: An axiomatic approach.* Columbus, OH: Charles E. Merrill Publishing Co., 1961.

ADDITIONAL REFERENCES

Morrison, P. *The curriculum triangle and its style* (Educational Services Quarterly Report). Cambridge, MA: Educational Services, Summer-Fall, 1964.

VanTassel-Baska, J. *An experimental study on the teaching of Latin to verbally precocious youth.* Unpublished doctoral dissertation, University of Toledo, 1982.

5

Identification and Assessment of the Gifted and Talented

John Feldhusen
Leland Baska

Identification of gifted and talented youth is a process through which we attempt to become aware of students whose abilities, motivational patterns, self-concepts, and creative capabilities are so far above average that differentiated educational services are needed if they are to make the full educational progress indicated by their potential (Brandwein, 1980). We assume that all youth have a right to educational services that will meet their needs, be adapted to their personal characteristics, and help them achieve to the highest possible level of their potential. Identification systems that merely enable us to label or categorize "gifted" youth are of no value, and potentially even harmful. The sole purpose of identification is to guide the educational process and serve youth.

The identification process has gone astray in many schools (Alvino, McDonnel, & Richert, 1981), especially when identification becomes an end in itself. In other schools educational services for the gifted are severely limited or nonexistent. Additionally, the identification process can exacerbate problems of elitism. We propose in this chapter to review some of the major issues and concerns related to identification and assessment, to suggest some methods of dealing with those issues, and to present a general set of guidelines for the identification and assessment processes.

SOME ISSUES AND CONCERNS

Validity and Appropriateness

A major issue related to identification is validity with respect to program goals and services. The identification process must be appropriate for selecting youth who need and will profit from a particular program service. The Future Problem Solving Program (Flack & Feldhusen, 1983) is one example of an excellent service offered in many gifted programs. Verbal skills and abilities, a high degree of motivation, creative capacity, and good independent study skills might be seen as appropriate abilities and characteristics of youth who need and would profit from that program. A valid identification process, then, would include assessment of the nominee's strengths in each of those areas. Assessment of math and science abilities as represented in standardized achievement test scores would be less relevant and could render the process invalid. Similarly, the use of language achievement tests and creativity and study skill scores to identify youth for accelerated algebra classes might be equally questionable. In summary, the identification process should select those youth whose needs, abilities, and characteristics fit the goals or nature of the program service to be offered.

We think that some programs at the early childhood level might identify *generally* gifted children who can profit from a general set of stimulating educational experiences. As children move through the elementary grades, however, their talents begin to crystallize in specific areas. Increasing attention must be paid to an individual's abilities and characteristics, matching them to appropriate and valid educational experiences.

Parent Input

Another issue of concern in identification of the gifted is parent input to the process. There is a myth that *all* parents think their children are gifted. In truth, few parents want to label their children as gifted. Nevertheless, parents do have a great amount of knowledge that is relevant to the identification process. They do not know the technical jargon of the gifted field, but they do know a great deal about the abilities, motivation, self-concept, and creative capacity of their children. Furthermore, they see their children in free behavior situations and less restrictive environments than the classroom. They often have information of which teachers are totally unaware, which can be extremely valuable in the identification process. Through rating scales, questionnaires, or open-ended instruments, parents can provide information concerning their children's reading habits, vocabulary, hobbies, interests, motivation, creative behavior, and self-views. All of this information can be valuable in the identification process. The *ASSETS* scale developed at Grand Rapids, Michigan, is one published example of an instrument to gain parent input in identification (*ASSETS*, 1979).

Combining Assessment Data

A major challenge in identification comes about when those who are carrying out the identification process wish to combine data from several sources for a unitary or synthesized evaluation of the child. Obviously, scores derived from different types of scales (e.g., percentiles, IQs, stanines, and Z scores) cannot simply be added together. Must we settle simply for a subjective, intuitive combination?

One answer, widely applied in the gifted field, is a simplified standardization process as represented in a matrix. All the scores are converted to a simple five-level or 10-level scale without regard to the variance of individual measures, and then summed to derive a gross index of giftedness. Feldhusen, Baska, and Womble (1981) have detailed the serious weaknesses of such matrix approaches and argued that a standardized score approach be used instead. They advocate that all input variables be converted to T scores and then combined, as a more reliable way of synthesizing data.

One-Shot vs. Continuing Assessment

Identification is often viewed as a one-time process, particularly if it seeks simply to identify, label, and categorize youth as gifted or non-gifted. Developmental psychology and the common sense of school personnel, however, indicate that children grow and children change. Most assuredly, their talents and abilities are undergoing processes of differentiation and specialization as they move through the elementary grades and into high school. Thus, the identification process demands yearly reassessment.

Yearly reassessment should not be oriented to the question of whether the child is *still* gifted. Rather, it should seek to identify changing abilities or characteristics and the emergence of more specialized talent or ability. Further, it should ask whether the student has special needs, related to the area(s) of talent or giftedness, for which new or different educational services are needed.

Reliability

The reliability of test scores, rating scales, observation data, and other measures used in assessing gifted youth varies tremendously. Some degree of imprecision is always present. Scores derived from intelligence and achievement tests are likely to be highly reliable. Other measures, such as nominating procedures, rating scales, creativity tests, and self-concept inventories, are likely to be low or very low in reliability. Thus, if the assessment is repeated or done by another examiner, the scores may differ substantially.

Information regarding the reliability and validity of standardized tests is available from the published test manual and the *Mental Measurement Yearbooks* (Buros, 1982). For rating scales, self-concept inventories, and observation systems, however, such information often is not even available.

Thus, users of any such instruments should make an effort to secure their own reliability estimates through test-retest, split-half, or interrater-interscorer analyses. Knowing the reliability of tests or other assessment procedures enables one to estimate identification-assessment scores for accuracy in the identification process. Procedures for estimating the reliability of several test or rating scores combined are presented by Nunnaly (1978, p. 248).

Ceiling Effect and Off-Grade Level Testing

When the form of the test for a child's age level is too easy or does not give the child a chance to show the full range of his or her ability, the ceiling effect may be operating. A well-known solution to this problem is the procedure called "off-grade level testing." In this procedure a level of test higher than the child's age or grade level is selected; this is hoped to be sufficiently challenging so that the child will have an opportunity to display the highest level of his or her ability.

Thousands of children now participate in off-grade testing at the middle school or junior high level by taking the *Scholastic Aptitude Test,* an instrument not ordinarily administered until the junior or senior year of high school (Sawyer, 1982). Presumably the test will be at such a high level that these younger students will all be able to display their highest levels of ability. Even in this form of radical off-grade testing, however, a few youngsters score at the perfect (800) level. They seemingly need an even higher form of off-grade test to adequately assess their talents and abilities.

Evaluation Procedures

Does the identification process select youth properly? Does it identify boys and girls who need special gifted program services? Will those who are selected do well in the special programs? Will those who are selected go on to high level success in their life careers? Will they go on to college and to advanced degrees? These are questions we must answer through research, evaluation, and dissemination procedures. Often, the identification process is taken for granted, and educators assume that it is selecting the students who can benefit most from the program.

In reality the identification process ought to undergo periodic validity evaluation. This should be done to determine if the process is bringing into the program the youth who have need for its services, especially those who will profit and grow as a result of receiving the services, and who will go on to use their potential to achieve at levels commensurate with their superior ability. These procedures involve gathering data concerning performance or achievement of youth in the program, and data on students' achievements after they leave the program. Do they go on to college, to graduate training, to advanced degrees, to significant achievement in their fields?

Identification procedures may also fail to bring in to the program youth who need its services, who would perform well, and who would achieve high level success if given the opportunity. A variety of assessment supplements and experimentation can be used to get at this issue, but the problem is not easily dealt with by school personnel. Coordinators of programs, however, should be aware of the situation and attempt to minimize its dangers by vigilance in searching for and assessing potentially gifted youth.

Performance or Potential?

The process of identifying gifted and talented youth is based primarily on current assessments of how well the youths are performing in tasks relevant to the areas of giftedness and talent. *All* test procedures are measures of *performance;* they are *not* measures of some hidden, innate, or basic capacity. All of the tasks included in intelligence and aptitude tests involve learned behaviors. Nevertheless, two kinds of inferences are often made from the tests. First, intelligence test scores sometimes *are* inferred as an index to innate capacity. Second, test scores such as those yielded by the *Scholastic Aptitude Test* are considered by some as an indicator or prediction of how well a student will learn or perform some time in the future.

The point to be made is that *all assessments of ability or aptitude are measures of current performance levels* and that their major value is in identifying youth who might profit from special gifted program services and go on to higher level success and achievement. Interpretation of test scores as representing innate abilities leads to misconceptions of giftedness as fixed and unchanging. Realistically, however, without nurture abilities may decline, while with nurture they may increase. Identifiers of gifted and talented youth must develop an understanding of the nature and uses of ability and aptitude scores and use them properly in the identification process.

Tryout as Identification

The identification process cannot achieve perfect reliability, primarily because it cannot be more reliable than the tests, rating scales, and observation data on which it is based. To counteract the dangers of low reliability in identification procedures, program coordinators should view tryout in programs as an extension of the identification process and offer tryout opportunities to as many borderline youth as possible.

Observation of students' performance in programs can provide valuable supplementary information to assess potential giftedness. Performance or learning in programs is one of the major criteria for evaluating identification predictors. Youth who can perform well in a program are most directly demonstrating one desired criterion for gifted programs. The identification process is a special case of predictive validity that should be tested against the criterion of the program. To the extent that students succeed, we can be sure of good predictive validity.

THE NATURE OF GIFTEDNESS

Parents and teachers often erroneously believe that administration of tests and other measures will result in explicit identification of youth as gifted and talented, or not gifted. Gifted youth are often perceived as being categorically different human beings, much like our classification of those who have diseases or handicaps. Thus, parents and teachers have been heard to ask if a particular child who seems to be precocious or bright is "really and truly gifted." The question seems to imply that some individuals are geniuses, others are pseudo-gifted, and if tested, rated, and observed properly, a gifted child will be clearly seen as gifted.

In truth, all types of giftedness and talent correspond to psychological characteristics and abilities that are continuous variables. The characteristics exist at some level in all human beings; they vary in intensity or level in each; and the abilities differ within each gifted individual. Thus, all living persons have some level of intelligence, as well as some adaptability, some ability in numerical or quantitative operations, and some ability for reasoning.

But some youth can reason rapidly and accurately with complex, abstract material, while others have limited reasoning capacity, can deal only with simple, concrete material, and are slow in reasoning. Furthermore, some youth have high mathematical reasoning ability but limited ability in verbal reasoning tasks, and vice versa. And they differ in levels of different abilities within themselves. The identification process must take these conditions into account.

PROPOSED IDENTIFICATION PROCEDURES

Procedures for identifying the gifted and talented must be closely linked to the nature of the program services, as discussed earlier in this chapter. Talents differ, assessment procedures differ, and different program services tap different talents. In the broadest sense, elementary program services differ in their mathematical, verbal, or artistic orientation. Later, as youth move into junior high and high school, talents become quite specialized in science, mathematics, languages, literature, social studies, music, art, dance, and so on (Saunders, 1982). The identification process must increasingly recognize specialization of talent and "fine tune" the identification process to fit the talent domain of a potentially gifted youth.

Nomination-Screening

The initial stage of identification may simply consist of a call for informal nominations. Parents, teachers, counselors, and gifted youth themselves would be invited to submit the names of students they view as gifted or talented. Before requesting nominations, some instruction concerning the nature and characteristics of the gifted and talented is desirable, so that nominators will have an accurate understanding of the type of youth being sought (Borland, 1978). Rating scales can also provide guidance to nominators, by focusing on salient characteristics of those nominees. Rating scales, however, are often not used until a second stage, after initial nomination procedures have been completed and have generated a pool for further assessment.

Further screening can be carried out through examination of *available* test scores in school files. IQ, reading readiness, and standardized achievement tests are typically found in the files. An inspection of those files can serve to identify students in the top 5–10 percent. These names, along with the file scores, can be added to the existing list of nominees.

The processes of securing nominations from relevant persons and from school files yield a list of nominees, many of whom are repeatedly mentioned. A particular child might be nominated by two teachers, the parents, and a counselor, as well as by having high IQ and achievement test scores. The greater the number of nomination sources, the greater is our confidence that a youth is indeed talented and merits further consideration. If resources permit, however, all youth who have at least one nomination source should be assessed.

Assessment

The next stage in the identification process is to secure additional information that will aid in determining the youth's talents or giftedness and his or her fit with particular services. Tests, rating scales, and other observations should be selected to match the potential abilities of the youth and the nature of the program services.

For a pullout program in which students will receive instruction related to the language arts, creativity, research, and independent study, the following data might logically be secured:

1. Language arts standardized achievement test scores.
2. Teacher ratings of the child's reading and writing skills.
3. Motivation assessment using the motivation scale developed by Renzulli, Smith, White, Callahan, & Hartman (1976).
4. Creativity assessment, using the *Torrance Tests of Creative Thinking* (1974).

For a leadership and personal-social development program, the following data might be secured:

1. A self-concept scale.
2. The Renzulli leadership rating scale (Renzulli et al., 1976).
3. IQ from a group test.
4. Sociogram information.

For an accelerated mathematics program, the following two items might be particularly applicable:

1. *Scholastic Aptitude Test* (College Board, n.d.) scores taken in seventh grade.
2. Mathematics achievement test scores.

Assessment should typically focus within two or more of the four domains of psychological functioning that relate to giftedness: (1) talents and abilities, (2) creative capacity, (3) self-concept, and (4) motivation. Test instruments are used to assess many talents and abilities, but some talents, especially in the arts, are typically assessed through expert judgment of students' performance or products. Creative capacity may be assessed using test instruments or rating scales. Self-concept is usually assessed using self-rating inventories such as the Piers-Harris scale (1969) or the *Me Scale* (Feldhusen & Kolloff, 1981). Motivation can be rated with one of the Renzulli scales (Renzulli et al., 1976), or it can be inferred from achievements or products that the nominee has produced.

Assessment of intelligence is often carried out with children at the elementary school level with the *Wechsler Intelligence Scale for Children–Revised* (1974) or the *Stanford-Binet Intelligence Scale* (Terman & Merrill, 1973). Assessment of general intelligence is most appropriate with children at the early childhood, primary, and upper grade levels in cases where the program is a broad, general instructional service. Intelligence tests are also used in making decisions concerning early admission or grade advancement.

Valuable assessment information can also be secured through interviews and from essays written by nominees. From essays, inferences can be drawn concerning writing skills, interests, and motivation. Essays were used in a career education project for the gifted (Moore, Feldhusen, & Owings, 1978) to assess the motivation and goals of nominees. They were asked to write a paper setting forth their own short- and long-range personal goals. In the same project, nominees were interviewed to assess their oral verbal abilities, social poise, and motivation/enthusiasm.

Combining Data

All the data from tests, rating scales, product assessment, interviews, and the like should be drawn together into a folder for each nominee. Scores relevant to a particular program service for which a nominee is being considered should be standardized, preferably by conversion to T scores. They can then be added together, weighted (if there is a rationale for increasing or reducing the power of each score in the combination), and a total score derived. Feldhusen, Baska, and Womble (1981) offer a detailed plan for combining standardized scores.

In some instances, program assignments might be made on the basis of a single test score. For example, children may be selected for an accelerated mathematics program on the basis of the mathematics score from the *Scholastic Aptitude Test.* In this case, the single score is highly relevant to the area of program service.

Diagnostic-Assessment Committee

Final decision making and selection of youth for program services should be a professional judgment. It should be dictated neither by a test score alone nor by some total or combination score. The cut-off level can be established, and for youth who score well above that level, the committee's decision may be perfunctory. For all the scores that cluster above and below the cut-off level, but within the standard error of measurement for these scales, committee judgment is necessary. In reaching a decision, the committee can take into account any other possibly relevant information. While relatively subjective, the committee's decision should nevertheless be based on sound professional judgment with due regard to the potential errors or lack of reliability in all of the assessment-identification procedures.

In some instances the committee can make a decision for tryout of a possibly gifted youth in a program service. This is often the case when youth are being selected for early admission or grade advancement. When doubt or uncertainty exists, the trial period should determine if the student can handle the demands of the new assignment and profit from the experience.

Continuing Student Evaluation as Identification

Students who have been placed in a program service [e.g., a full-time self-contained class, a pullout program, an accelerated math class, an Advanced Placement (College Board, 1983) class, or a future problem solving program] should be evaluated periodically to determine their progress and ascertain if the identification decision was sound. Are they progressing well? Does the service meet some of their needs? The diagnostic-identification committee should receive this type of information periodically (e.g., every six to nine weeks), and the committee should make decisions concerning the desirability of a gifted youth's continuation in the program, withdrawal, or reassignment to another program service.

Repeated evaluation to determine if a child is gifted or not seems to be of little value. The critical issue is determining if the child has continuing special educational needs that cannot be served in a regular classroom, and whether the special program service is meeting those needs.

SUMMARY

The purpose of the identification process in gifted education is to identify youth whose abilities, motivation, self-concept, interests, and creative talents are so far above average that special education program services are needed to meet their needs. All youth have a right to educational programs that will help them achieve their highest potential. Program services for the gifted should be designed to fit each child's unique characteristics and needs. Because parents know their own children better than anyone else, their input should be a vital part of the identification process.

This is really a continuing effort. It should not be viewed as a one-time assessment. Children's performance in a program should be used to verify or contradict the results of tests and rating scales administered. Reliability and validity of the tests and rating scales are crucial to the process. Giftedness is not a unique diagnostic category; rather, it denotes children whose abilities are markedly higher but not fundamentally different from other children.

In practice, identification of the gifted begins with a nomination–screening process that seeks to find all possibly gifted youth. An assessment process should follow in which various measures are secured to determine the levels of a youth's special talents and abilities. When all the data have been gathered, a diagnostic-assessment committee should review the data, determine whether each nominee has special needs because of the superior talent or ability, and suggest appropriate educational service. Programs for gifted students should consist of a variety of services that can be used selectively to fit their special characteristics and needs.

REFERENCES

Alvino, J., McDonnel, R.C., & Richert, S. National survey of identification practices in gifted and talented education. *Exceptional Children,* 1981, *48,* 124-132.

ASSETS. *User's guide to A.S.S.E.T.S.* Holmers Beach, FL: Learning Publications, 1979.

Borland, J. Teacher identification of the gifted. *Journal for the Education of the Gifted,* 1978, *2,* 22-32.

Brandwein, P.R. On the search for the gifted. *Roeper Review,* 1980, *3,* 2-3.

Buros, O.K. *Eighth mental measurement yearbook.* Highland Park, NJ: College Board Publications, 1982.

College Board. *A guide to the advanced placement program.* New York: Author, 1983.

College Board. *10 SATs: Scholastic aptitude tests of the College Board.* New York: Author, n.d.

Feldhusen, J.F., Baska, L.K., & Womble, S.R. Using standard scores to synthesize data in identifying the gifted. *Journal for the Education of the Gifted,* 1981, *4,* 177-185.

Feldhusen, J.F., & Kolloff, M.B. ME: A self concept scale for gifted students. *Perceptual & Motor Skills,* 1981, *53,* 319-323.

Flack, J.D., & Feldhusen, J.F. Future studies in the curricular framework of the Purdue three-stage model. *G/C/T,* March/April 1983, *27.*

Moore, B.A., Feldhusen, J.F., & Owings, J. *Professional career exploration program for minority and/or low income gifted and talented high school students.* West Lafayette, IN: Education Department, Purdue University, 1978.

Nunnaly, J.C. *Psychometric theory.* New York: McGraw-Hill, 1978, p. 248.

Piers, E.V.; & Harris, D.B. *The Piers-Harris Children's self-concept scale.* Nashville, TN: Counselor Recordings and Tests, 1969.

Renzulli, J.S., Smith, L.H., White, A.J., Callahan, C.M., & Hartman, R.K. *Scales for rating the behavioral characteristics of superior students.* Wethersfield, CT: Creative Learning Press, 1976.

Saunders, R.J. Screening and identifying the talented in art. *Roeper Review,* 1982, *4,* 7-10.

Sawyer, R.N. The Duke University program to identify and educate brilliant young students. *Journal for the Education of the Gifted,* 1982, *5,* 185-189.

Terman, L., & Merrill, M. *Stanford-Binet intelligence scale.* Boston: Houghton Mifflin, 1973.

Torrance, E.P. *Torrance tests of creative thinking.* Bensenville, IL: Scholastic Testing Service, 1974.

Wechsler, D. *Wechsler intelligence scale for children–revised.* New York: Psychological Corp., 1974.

Key Administrative Concepts in Gifted Program Development

Joyce VanTassel-Baska

In many respects, administrative arrangements such as grouping, articulation, and cost effectiveness are superficial issues in the education of the gifted. Yet, when those arrangements have little or no flexibility, they begin to account for substantive problems that gifted students may encounter. In examining administrative arrangements, then, it may be helpful to think of them as being either facilitative or impedimentive as they impinge on the lives of gifted students.

KEY CONCEPT #1: GROUPING

The importance of finding an appropriate peer group or at least one significant other for the emotional development of the gifted is well documented (Gowan, 1964; Gowan & Bruch, 1971; Colangelo & Zaffrann, 1979; Silverman, 1983). And high level and extensive cognitive functioning is facilitated by a core group of intellectual peers with similar goals (Terman, 1921; Hollingworth, 1942; Hall, 1956; Keating, 1976). Thus, it is understandable that grouping of the gifted has always been advocated in some form by educators of the gifted.

Certainly in terms of the historical context of gifted programs since the early 1900s, those that have been the most effective and the longest running clearly have been the programs with full-time grouping as the underlying strategy. These programs include the Hollingworth schools in New York City, the Terman classes in St. Louis, San Diego, and other cities, and the Cleveland Major Work Program. At the secondary level, the Bronx High School of Science in New York City and the Walnut Hills High School in Cincinnati are both examples of the success of this approach.

Not only is the cognitive development of these students enhanced by grouping arrangements, but also the affective development in terms of their social and emotional growth in a context where others have similar interests and abilities. Numerous case studies point up that students who have been in a full-time grouping arrangement feel that they have benefited greatly. One example is Bob Sharpe, president of Bell and Howell, who testified that his involvement in the Major Work Program led him to have the confidence and perceptiveness to be able to rise to the presidency of that corporation (Hauck & Freehill, 1972). Another argument for the full-time grouping approach is that it represents tremendous benefits to the organization of the school because it is an integrative program run at no additional cost to the system.

Yet, little empirical evidence specifies the exact beneficial effects of grouping versus non-grouping among populations of gifted students. The lack of evidence relates partially to the difficulty of controlling variables and isolating the treatment of grouping as a single variable in any design chosen. It also relates to the logistical difficulty of organizing such a research effort in a school setting where the dictates of the study involve withholding treatment that is perceived as important to the development of all children identified as gifted.

General Research on Ability Grouping

Ability grouping is defined differentially from study to study, school to school, district to district. Procedurally, groups are often divided within the classroom, sometimes more broadly within the institution, sometimes categorized by specific subject area, other times, not.

Methodology for Group Selection
Methodologically, aptitude is determined in different ways. Sometimes it is determined on the basis of selective test scores or prior achievement in a given academic area (e.g., math), other times on the basis of overall standardized achievement tests, and often on the basis of teacher recommendations.

Outcome Variables
Measured outcomes differ from study to study. Some are concerned with self-concept, others with friendship patterns, attitude toward subject matter and school, others with achievement results themselves.

The literature with regard to ability grouping is also characterized by methodological flaws. Internal validity is not always controlled for. "In cases where homogeneous or heterogeneous ability grouping is related to improved scholastic performance, the curriculum is subject to substantial modification of teaching methods, materials and other variables which are intrinsic to the teaching-learning process, and which, therefore, may well be the causative factors related to academic development wholly apart from ability grouping per se" (Findley & Bryan, 1970, p. 16).

Pros and Cons of Ability Grouping

Arguments do exist in the literature to support ability grouping in general. Homogeneous grouping (1) allows students to advance at their own rate with others of similar ability, (2) offers students methods and materials geared to their level, (3) provides a challenge for students to excel or to be promoted to the next level within a realistic range of competition, and (4) makes teaching easier by restricting the range (Esposito, 1971; Morrison, 1976).

The cons of ability grouping include the usual arguments that (1) ability grouping is undemocratic and affects the self-concept of all children adversely by placing a stigma on those in lower groups while giving higher group children an inflated sense of their self-worth, (2) most adult life experiences do not occur in homogeneous settings and students must learn to work with a wide range of people, (3) students of lesser ability may profit from learning with those of greater ability, (4) ability grouping tends to segregate children along ethnic, socioeconomic lines as well as ability lines, and (5) achieving truly homogeneous grouping even along a single achievement variable is impossible because test data represent only one type of distinction among varying patterns of individual differences (Findley & Bryan, 1970).

American education has found more comfort in assuming responsibility for socializing children than for meeting their unique educational needs. The issue of grouping conflicts with this overarching socialization goal, for its rationale is educational, based on the psychological differences inherent among children with respect to learning at any given stage of their development. Thus, social role behavior has become embedded in the dilemma of whether to group children according to ability, and in the last 20 years has taken precedence over the educational issues involved. Thus, comparing the rationale for and against ability grouping and noting the lack of definitive research, it is reasonable to concur with Morrison's (1976) sense that "grouping practices have been determined by social and political rather than by purely educational considerations" (p. 67).

Research on Positive Effects of Grouping Gifted Students

One study suggested that the heterogeneity of students' entering achievement levels in a given class limits the teacher's successful adaptation of instruction to individual students' academic needs (Evertson, Sanford, & Emmer, 1981). More heterogeneity was also associated with a lesser degree of student task engagement and cooperation. The researchers also cautioned that heterogeneous grouping places unusual demands on teachers, particularly in the area of classroom management skills.

The Findley and Bryan research review (1970) noted that grouping within a classroom for instruction in particular subjects was an accepted and commended practice, and that achievement grouping by individual subjects may be used to advantage. Several studies point to somewhat positive results or effects of ability grouping within specific subjects. In a controlled study of 360 seventh and eighth graders, a computation test revealed better performance by those who were assigned to one of three ability levels on the basis of academic achievement and teachers' recommendations than those who were not (Adamson, 1971).

On the basis of a review of the empirical literature on ability grouping for math instruction, Begle (1975) recommended that school systems should be encouraged to experiment with grouping students within the classroom, and that research on team teaching should be done. He mentioned that in math there is "little evidence to indicate that students at one ability level benefit from the presence of students at other ability levels" (p. 9). The Study for Mathematically Precocious Youth (SMPY) Project, in operation since 1971, continues to report positive results from highly selective grouping strategies (Stanley, Keating, & Fox, 1974; Keating, 1976).

With regard to achievement, positive results were obtained from grouping in the Illinois Gifted Experimental Study (Bent, 1969). According to Justman (1965), "the segregation of intellectually gifted pupils in a special class is generally accompanied by academic achievement superior to that normally attained by equally gifted pupils who remain in normal progress groups."

Provus (1970) studied 494 students in grades 4–6 in Homewood, Illinois, grouped homogeneously for math only. On the basis of results of the arithmetic concepts subtest of the *Iowa Tests of Basic Skills,* Provus concluded that "children at all ability levels, grouped by ability, were more familiar with arithmetic concepts and fundamentals than children not grouped by ability." Also, the academically talented students profited most from ability grouping, the average students profited slightly, and the slow students profited no more from homogeneous grouping than they did from heterogeneous grouping.

Kulik and Kulik (1982) recently employed meta-analysis to review the empirical literature on ability grouping. They found that students gained somewhat more from grouped classes than from ungrouped ones. The benefits were slight but existent in the area of achievement, with an average increase of one-tenth of a standard deviation on achievement exams. The special honors programs often had beneficial effects on the performance of gifted and talented students (p. 426).

Research also tends to support the positive attitudinal effects of grouping gifted students, noting that high ability students benefited from the stimulation of other high ability students, and from the special curricula (Kulik & Kulik, 1982, p. 426).

Wilcox (1963) studied 1,157 eighth grade students to determine the multiple effects of grouping upon their growth and behavior. He found that, for the total group, self-concept and attitude toward school were unrelated to grouping, but low ability groups had a more positive self-concept and attitude toward school with homogeneous grouping.

It seems safe to conclude that research data on the positive effects of grouping gifted students are sufficiently favorable to recommend grouping strategies based on the academic needs of gifted students as such needs can be diagnosed for follow-up educational intervention.

Why Group the Gifted?

Being caught in the crossfire of conflicting educational philosophies on grouping can be a major detriment to the academic development of gifted students. Even when a classroom has been purposely devised as heterogeneous, in reality teachers either group within such a schema to deliver instruction appropriately to different learning levels or they lower the overall instructional level to ensure total group understanding. In both cases, grouping has occurred.

The real question seems to center on the purpose for which grouping is done. If it is done to segregate students by income, race, or sex, it should not be tolerated in a public school context. But if it is done to facilitate instruction at appropriate levels, it is indeed meritorious and merely formalizes at a different level (i.e., the classroom) what individual teachers have done within heterogeneous classrooms in the name of individualized instruction.

Figure 4 presents four grouping strategies: heterogeneous classroom, pullout, semi-separation, and homogeneous classroom. Each grouping arrangement has possible effects, both positive and negative, for educational planners to consider. The key to decision making on this issue must rest with the overall educational purpose of the school as perceived by its administration, board, and community. Are efficient institutional approaches too costly in other dimensions? What is the school's primary purpose? Can both academic concerns and social concerns be accommodated through a choice of grouping models?

If one examines the possible effects of a given grouping strategy on gifted students, as illustrated in Figure 4, it becomes clear that the more they are grouped in terms of contact time, the more their unique educational needs are met; and conversely, the less they are grouped, the more likely those needs will not be met in any organized and systematic way. Thus, full-time grouping for the gifted should be strongly considered by any school whose primary purpose is perceived to be the development of individual potential.

Strategies for Accomplishing Full-Time Grouping

Full-time grouping of the gifted for academic purposes within the context of a school or district can be handled in various ways. A separate classroom within a school building is perhaps

FIGURE 4
Range of Grouping Strategies

Heterogeneous Classroom (no formal grouping of the gifted)	Pullout Grouping Arrangement (3 hours or less per week)	Semi-Separation (5–15 hours per week)	Full-time Grouping (homogeneous classroom)
Possible Positive Effects	*Possible Positive Effects*	*Possible Positive Effects*	*Possible Positive Effects*
• potential for social interaction with all ability ranges • development of tutorials to help "slower" students • development of independent work habits	• some access to appropriate curriculum • some contact with intellectual peers • more group work with intellectual peers	• opportunity to address academic strengths • potential for social adaptation in both settings • rewarding peer contacts	• maximum opportunity to develop intellectual peer group • potential for appropriate and integrated curriculum • opportunities for classroom work in small groups that share abilities and interests
Possible Negative Effects	*Possible Negative Effects*	*Possible Negative Effects*	*Possible Negative Effects*
• no organized ability peer group • less challenging curriculum • student *always* working independently to achieve appropriate level	• fragmentation of curriculum • heightened awareness of being labeled "gifted"	• lack of group identification • difficulty in integrating the curriculum • problems associated with being labeled "gifted"	• development of insensitivity to non-gifted students • development of self-concept based on perceptions of ability rather than total person

the most common approach at the elementary level. In schools where this strategy is employed, gifted students participate with all other age-mates for physical education, lunch, and both art and music periods. Another strategy used successfully is cross-age/cross-grade grouping, especially in small schools where each grade level does not have enough gifted students to establish a class. In that arrangement, a primary classroom for the gifted might contain children from age 4 to age 7 or 8, working at fifth and sixth grade levels in basic skill areas.

Still another strategy is to establish academic periods, already commonly found in middle schools and high schools, during which students of similar ability study the various content fields offered. Usually the academic period approach carries with it some disadvantages such as (1) fragmentation of learning into visibly separate content fields, (2) the use of several teachers to deliver instruction, thereby limiting opportunities for curriculum integration and knowing individual students well, and (3) a certain regimentation of scheduling.

Nevertheless, any or all of these strategies can be used effectively to bring about an instructional delivery system that will facilitate the education of gifted students. Developing a delivery system for grouping the gifted is crucial to good program development practice and also to the individual student, for each individual needs a sufficiently challenging context in which to experience growth.

KEY CONCEPT #2: PROGRAM ARTICULATION

Any discussion of the issue of program articulation at a time when many programs are just beginning and others are working to maintain themselves seems rather presumptuous, but the issue of program articulation is central to meaningful program development practices (Tyler, 1958). The term "program articulation" refers to development of appropriate offerings for gifted students on a K–12 basis, with planned curriculum experiences that allow for progressive development of both content and process skills. To examine the issue intelligently, however, we must look at necessary components in the educational enterprise that affect schools' ability to carry out such efforts.

Components of Articulation

One of the assumptions that underlies the ability to carry out program articulation is that schools are willing to accept a primary role for developing individual academic potential. To implement an articulation plan effectively, schools must modify their basic educational program to meet the academic needs of gifted students. In so doing, they must be willing to abandon a chronological age basis for determining curriculum skill levels and examine instead a *competency-based model* for progress. (Though many educators purport to employ a continuous progress model, in reality it is usually related to steps taken for slower students only.)

A second ingredient of good program articulation is that identification of gifted children occurs when they enter the school district, usually at kindergarten level. The argument frequently given for not identifying at this age is that the tests available to measure giftedness are not reliable or valid for such young children. Several recent studies (Roedell, Jackson, & Robinson, 1980; VanTassel-Baska, Schuler, & Lipschutz, 1982) have indicated, however, that several effective tools can be used in combination for successful identification of young children. Obviously, no identification system at entry will identify all gifted children who could profit from later programming, so provision for an ongoing identification procedure is essential. But from the articulation perspective, *early programming* is critical for ensuring appropriate skill development and commensurate excitation for learning.

A third component underlying articulation is that schools must have some provision for *grouping* gifted children together in the academic areas. Carrying out an articulated program with gifted students who are not seen frequently or for reasonable periods of time is almost impossible. Thus, effective grouping must be employed to make an articulation plan workable.

Another aspect of program articulation is the need for *self-pacing* of the gifted in the core content areas in which the program is offered. A euphemism for self-pacing in the field of education of the gifted is content acceleration and modification, in which scope and sequence in reading, mathematics, science, and social studies for gifted students is effected from kindergarten through the secondary level. Especially important, given the learning rate differences and intellectual power of gifted students, is the use of (1) a diagnostic/prescriptive approach over time to assure that the learning is progressive, (2) a conceptually organized curriculum that compresses content into major schemas, systems, and matrices for ease in mastering important knowledge areas, and (3) a teacher who facilitates and monitors progress in relationship to student mastery.

An articulation plan also has to address the *integration of process skills, special projects, mentorships, internships, and other modifications* of the overall curriculum for these students into the traditional subject matter provided within the context of the school. Working on the process skills within the traditional domains of knowledge to ensure that gifted students both master them and are able to transfer that mastery to applicable areas makes the most sense.

Assumptions about Teachers and Teaching

Program articulation carries certain assumptions about the selection and training procedures for teachers who work with gifted students. To facilitate conceptual learning in the gifted, the teacher must understand a given domain of knowledge well enough to organize it effectively for able learners and be able to develop advanced level work for which they may be ready early. Even elementary teachers of the gifted need good content mastery so they can work effectively with the gifted in these areas. Selecting a teacher to work with the mathematically gifted, then, would require high-level ability and training in mathematics, as well as demonstrated effectiveness with gifted students at a given age level. A differentiated staffing pattern within the traditional elementary school could be an effective strategy for obtaining appropriate staff for such programs.

Finally, program articulation implies a sustained confluent approach to meeting the needs of the gifted population. The strategies of acceleration, enrichment, and counseling all have their part in the delivery of an appropriate program effort. A carefully conceived long-range plan that incorporates all of these issues can be effected in any school district that is willing to expend the effort on behalf of gifted students.

KEY CONCEPT #3: COST EFFECTIVENESS

Programs for the gifted may be entering a new cycle in regard to how educators perceive their benefits. More than ever before, cost effectiveness is an issue in educational programming. Because of general cuts in educational funding at federal, state, and local levels, special programs, including those for the gifted, are being examined more critically.

First, what constitutes an effective gifted program? There are perhaps two ways to respond to that question. One is to cite limited research available on the evaluation of gifted programs (Gallagher, Weiss, Oglesby, & Thomas, 1982). Another is to cite the standards used to judge programs exemplary on a state-wide basis (*Illinois Exemplary Program Handbook,* 1979). To be judged effective by the first approach, a program must demonstrate specific benefits to students in the areas of cognitive and/or affective growth. Few programs have found their way into the literature through such an evaluative perspective. The one sustained evaluation effort in this area in the last 20 years is the work of the Study for Mathematically Precocious Youth (SMPY) at The Johns Hopkins University, where student growth gains have been impressive.

Standards for what constitutes an effective program for the gifted are more general, yet taken as a whole may be helpful in determining the issue of effectiveness. The standards used for identifying exemplary programs in the Illinois study were:

1. That identification of gifted students (a) focus on the top 5-8% of a school population, (b) use appropriate instrumentation based on the nature of the program planned, (c) utilize a balance between objective criteria such as tests and subjective criteria such as teacher recommendations and peer inventories, and (d) provide an ongoing process for inclusion of eligible students.

2. That the program have appropriate objectives and activities for the nature and needs of the population selected.

3. That teaching strategies stress the use of higher level thinking processes, problem solving techniques, discussions, and high quality student products.

4. That appropriate measures be taken to select and train the best teachers available for the specific program to be implemented, and that community resources be utilized.

5. That programs provide comprehensive articulation for students across grade levels and subject areas as need indicates.

6. That materials be selected and used in accordance with program objectives.

7. That the school and community demonstrate involvement with the program through regular interaction in activities such as parent education seminars, board meetings, and special workshops.

8. That the program evaluation be comprehensive, utilizing appropriate instrumentation to document student growth, attitudes of significant publics, and efficacy of program processes.

Classroom observation, interview, and review of pertinent documents (*Illinois Exemplary Program Handbook,* 1979) constituted the strategies used by the teams to ascertain if self-nominated school districts were operating exemplary gifted programs.

If these are reasonable standards to consider in finding a gifted program effective, what are the criteria to be used in assessing cost effectiveness? Since 80% of any program budget is allocated for personnel costs, a major issue to consider in keeping gifted program costs under control should be to have a plan for flexible use of existing human resources. Several strategies can be employed to heighten this possibility:

FIGURE 5
Some Examples of Low-Cost Gifted Programs

	Example Program A	Example Program B	Example Program C	Example Program D	Example Program E
Grouping Procedures	Shared instruction periods coordinated through individual education plans made by regular teachers	Cluster grouping of primary-level gifted students to a class: other students are also assigned	Part-time class of gifted children from a mixed grade grouping for grades 3–5	Separate course/class for gifted middle school students or cluster in class with other students	Individual mentorships or internships set up with community resource persons
Frequency of Contact	150 minutes per week for shared instruction; ongoing differentiated education in regular classroom	All day	1 hour per day or portion of 1 day per week (about 300 minutes total per week)	One class period or more per day depending upon student's needs	2 hours or more per week
Site	Each school: grades 4–6	Each school: grades 2–3	Each school: resource room, media center, etc.	Each school	Home studio or work site of mentor

Teaching Arrangement	All 4th–6th grade teachers plan together once a week for gifted students and arrange for a group contact time under leadership of teacher or other person	One regular primary teacher works with cluster of gifted and with other assigned students	Itinerant teacher or regular teachers freed for 1 hour per day to work with students	Junior high teacher conducts advanced instruction in subject as part of regular load	Students are given release time to pursue independent research generated by mentor or internship. School coordinator meets regularly with students and mentors to discuss progress
Resources Needed	Training of all teachers involved, plus materials	Aide, resource teacher, and/or volunteers to assist, plus training for teacher, plus materials	Training for teacher, plus a room or area to conduct class, plus materials	Training for teachers, plus some materials	Volunteer mentors, plus transportation to off-school sites, plus a coordinator to find mentors, match students, and monitor progress

Excerpted from *An Administrator's Guide to the Education of the Gifted and Talented* by J. VanTassel-Baska (Washington, DC: National Association of State Boards of Education, 1981).

- Grouping and scheduling
- Differentiated staffing
- Planned use of community volunteers
- Extended school day and year.

The examples of low-cost gifted programs given in Figure 5 employ these strategies to varying degrees.

SUMMARY

The administrative issues of grouping, program articulation, and cost effectiveness have been highlighted in this chapter because of their importance in structuring an effective program for gifted students within the context of current educational practice. No doubt, grouping decisions will continue to be made on philosophical and political bases, but an understanding of the educational implications of such decisions for gifted students is crucial. Programs that offer short-term services will continue to run, but an understanding of long-term linkages may short-circuit the proliferation of these models. And while some gifted programs may be able to ignore the trend for educational cost accountability, the majority will feel obligated to consider cost-effective measures that enhance rather than reduce program services.

Based on the discussion in this chapter, the need for effective administrative strategies in implementing gifted programs is critical to their success and longevity. Full-time grouping of gifted students is recommended to provide maximum benefits in both cognitive and affective areas. A plan for K–12 articulation of programs and services is suggested to enhance individual student development. And cost-effective strategies for sustaining educationally effective programs are strongly advocated.

REFERENCES

Adamson, D. *Differentiated multi-track grouping vs. uni-track educational grouping in mathematics.* Unpublished doctoral dissertation, Brigham Young University, 1971.

Begle, E.J. *Ability grouping for math instruction—A review of the empirical literature* (SMEG Working Paper No. 17). Stanford, CA: Stanford University, 1975.

Bent, L. *Grouping of the gifted—An experimental approach.* Peoria, IL: Bradley University, 1969.

Colangelo, N., & Zaffrann, R. *New voices in counseling the gifted.* Dubuque, IA: Kendall Hunt Publishers, 1979.

Esposito, D. *Homogeneous and heterogeneous grouping: Principal findings and implications of a re-search of the literature.* Bloomington, IN: Phi Delta Kappa Educational Foundation, 1971.

Evertson, C., Sanford, J., & Emmer, E. Effects of class heterogeneity in junior high school. *American Educational Research Journal,* 1981, *18*(2), 219-232.

Findley, W., & Bryan, M. *Ability grouping 1970: Status, impact and alternatives.* Atlanta, GA: Center for Educational Improvement, 1970.

Gallagher, J., Weiss, P., Oglesby, K., & Thomas, T. *Report on education of gifted, II.: Surveys of education of gifted students.* Chapel Hill, NC: Frank Porter Child Development Center, University of North Carolina, 1982.

Gowan, J.C. Twenty-five suggestions for parents of able children. *Gifted Child Quarterly,* 1964, *8*, 192-193.

Gowan, J., & Bruch, C.B. *The academically talented student and guidance.* Boston: Houghton Mifflin, 1971.

Hall, T. *Gifted children, the Cleveland story.* Cleveland: World Publishing Co., 1956.

Hauck, B.B., & Freehill, M.F. *Gifted case studies.* Dubuque, IA: William C. Brown, 1972.

Hollingworth, L. *Children above 180 I.Q.* New York: World Book Publishing Co., 1942.

Illinois Exemplary Program Handbook. Springfield, IL: Illinois Office of Education, 1979.

Justman, J. Academic achievement of intellectually gifted accelerants and non-accelerants in junior high school. *School Review,* 1965, *62*, 142-150.

Keating, D.P. (Ed.). *Intellectual talent: Research and development.* Baltimore: Johns Hopkins University Press, 1976.

Kulik, C.L., & Kulik, J. Effects of ability grouping on secondary school students: A meta-analysis of evaluation findings. *American Educational Research Journal,* 1982, *19*(3), 415-428.

Morrison, C.M. Ability grouping and mixed ability grouping in secondary schools. *Educational Issues Review 1.* Glasgow: Scottish Council for Research in Education, 1976.

Provus, M. Evaluation or research, research or evaluation. *Educational Technology,* 1970, *10*(8), 50-54.

Roedell, W., Jackson, N., & Robinson, H. *Gifted young children.* New York: Teachers College Press, 1980.

Silverman, L. The affective needs of gifted children. In J. VanTassel-Baska (Ed.), *A practical guide to counseling the gifted in a school setting.* Reston, VA: Council for Exceptional Children, 1983.

Stanley, J.C., Keating, D.P., & Fox, L.H. (Eds.). *Mathematical talent: Discovery, description, and development.* Baltimore: Johns Hopkins University Press, 1974.

Terman, L. (Ed.). *Genetic studies of genius* (Vol. 1). Stanford, CA: Stanford University Press, 1921.

Tyler, R. *Principles of curriculum and instruction.* Chicago: University of Chicago Press, 1958.

VanTassel-Baska, J. *An administrator's guide to the education of the gifted and talented.* Washington, DC: National Association of State Boards of Education (NASBE), 1981.

VanTassel-Baska, J., Schuler, A., & Lipschutz, J. An experimental program for gifted four-year-olds. *Journal for the Education of the Gifted,* 1982, *5*(1), 45-55.

Wilcox, J. *A search for the multiple effects of grouping upon the growth and behavior of junior high school pupils.* Unpublished doctoral dissertation, Cornell University, 1963.

ADDITIONAL REFERENCES

Ekstrom, R.B. Experimental studies of homogeneous grouping: A critical review. *School Review,* 1961, *69*, 216-226.

Gallagher, J. *Research summary on gifted children.* Springfield, IL: Department of Program development for Gifted Children, Office of Superintendent of Public Instruction, 1966.

Hoyle, E. The study of schools as organizations. In H.J. Butcher & H.B. Pont (Eds.), *Educational research in Britain.* London: University of London Press, 1973.

Kelly, A.V. *Mixed ability grouping—Theory and practice.* London: Harper & Row, 1978.

Papalia, A. Attitudes of students, teachers and administrators toward ability grouping for individualizing instruction. *Foreign Language Annals,* 1975, *8*(1), 54-55.

Stanley, J.C., & Benbow, C.P. (Eds.). *Academic precocity: Aspects of its development, consequences, and nurturance.* Baltimore: Johns Hopkins University Press, 1983.

Wilson, R., & Ribovich, J. Ability group? Stop and reconsider. *Reading World,* 1973, *13*(2), 81-91.

7

Facilitators for Gifted Learners

Ken Seeley

During the course of childhood, many significant persons impact on a child's development. In the case of gifted children, this array of significant people and the roles they play can have a great effect on the realization of their potential. These significant people involved in educating gifted children transcend formal education. In his landmark work, *Excellence,* Gardner (1961) stated:

> Education in the formal sense is only a part of the society's larger task of abetting the individual's intellectual, emotional and moral growth. What we must reach for is a conception of perpetual self-discovery, perpetual reshaping to realize one's best self, to be the person one could be. (p. 162)

In examining the role of significant persons in a gifted child's environment, this chapter addresses the facilitators of learning. It is limited to certain major groups with the realization that others not included might have a significant role. Possibly, Einstein would never have reached his potential had he not had an uncle who played mathematics games with him as a child. Or it might have been the nontraditional teachers influenced by Pestolozzi that Einstein had in a special school who stimulated his success. Rarely does only one facilitator make the difference in the realization of potential but, rather, a network of individuals who influence a child's learning both positively and negatively along with a good deal of chance factors.

With this selective view of facilitators, the discussion here will examine the roles of teachers, parents, mentors, and support personnel. Selection of the term "facilitators" is based on Gardner's premise of "perpetual self-discovery." An individual developmental concept, perpetual self-discovery can be facilitated but not created. The ultimate responsibility for learning must rest with the child. The facilitators, however, must be sensitive to learning. As Piaget (1970) stated:

> Remember also that each time one prematurely teaches a child something he could have discovered for himself, that child is kept from inventing it, and consequently from understanding it completely.

TEACHERS AS FACILITATORS

What are the Roots of Teacher Preparation For Gifted Learners?

The preparation of teachers in our country began with little awareness of the problems of special students. Modeled after the European pattern, knowledge of subject matter and criteria for mastery of content were key values for the first upper schools in our country. Teachers were academic specialists, and educational settings were highly competitive in nature (Wilson, 1958). This educational philosophy dominated the early years of our country and was

> ...only slightly affected either by the movement for the training of teachers that developed during the nineteenth century or by the anxiety of public schoolmen over the differences in learning ability among the children to be taught in the established system of free universal education. (p. 365)

While this emphasis was developing, the special needs of bright and able children were also surfacing. Pressures were mounting for academic accomplishment on the part of these pupils. Gallagher (1960) later stated this growing concern:

> The present nation-wide concern about the education of gifted children apparently stems from three main sources. First, there is the American educational tradition of being concerned with individual differences of all types and adapting to them. Second, there is the undeniable impact of world crises that helped us to become aware that the country's future is related to the educational future of these children. Third, there are the needs of a complex society for a vast reservoir of highly educated and intelligent leaders in the arts and sciences. (p. 1)

Tannenbaum (1979) postulated that the half-decade following Sputnik in 1957 and the last half of the 1970s might be viewed as peak periods of interest in gifted education. Between these peaks were only occasional bright spots for gifted and talented students and their potential teachers. Teacher preparation institutions for the most part reflected society's interest in low functioning, poorly motivated, and socially handicapped children.

This alternating or cyclical interest in the gifted was aptly described by Gardner (1961): "The critical lines of tension in our society are between emphasis on individual performance and restraints on individual performance" (p. 33). The conflict was rooted in society's dual commitment to excellence and equality in education. To foster excellence meant encouraging the gifted to work up to their potential ability, but if this necessitated special educational services or teachers, it was under fire for being elitist. Conversely, support for egalitarianism, while providing increased attention to the "lower status" students, threatened to deprive gifted students of full academic advantage to develop their own potentialities. "Perhaps because we cannot live exclusively with excellence or egalitarianism for any length of time and tend to counterpose rather than reconcile them, we seem fated to drift from one to the other indefinitely" (Tannenbaum, 1979, p. 6).

Teacher education institutions reflected this fleeting interest three decades ago. A 1951 survey of all teacher education institutions, conducted by Wilson (1953), attempted to determine the availability of gifted education courses. Of the 400 replies, 2% indicated "required" or "elective" special courses on gifted existing at the undergraduate level; and 5% reported courses in graduate programs. A little over half the responding universities stated that material dealing with the gifted was included in discussion of individual differences in courses such as education and child psychology, principles of education, and methods. Several universities utilized special summer session programs, particularly at the graduate level, to provide practicing teachers with courses in gifted education.

A follow-up study in 1956 revealed little change in the informal approach to teacher education for the gifted. Wilson (1958) summarized, "It seems doubtful that students by such limited attention are being supplied with the insights and skills suitable to the creative and potential natures of gifted and talented youth" (p. 367).

Davis (1954), Wilson (1958), and Snider (1960) found very few institutions offering a specific sequence of courses related to teaching the gifted. The programs at Kent State University, Hunter College, and Pennsylvania State University were exceptional at that time in that they included sequential coursework, advanced study, practica and graduate degree offerings.

Abraham's (1958) study reported that of 4,601 persons majoring in special education, only 21 persons were concentrating on the gifted child. Only two of the 1,549 who were awarded degrees in special education majored in gifted child education. Abraham also found that of the 897 higher education faculty members working in special education, one was devoting full time to gifted instruction. He indicated that a trend toward greater interest was shown by numerous dissertations being completed in this field. Gowan and Demos (1964) stated:

> One of the educational phenomena of our times which the future will find almost impossibly difficult to explain or account for is the almost total lack of attention to the selection and training of teachers of the gifted. (p. 382)

A more recent study conducted by Laird and Kowalski (1972) sought information regarding courses offered at 1,564 colleges and universities (with enrollment of 500 or more). Results showed that 151 (13%) of the institutions responding offered courses dealing specifically with education of the gifted; 11% of the respondents indicated that "Special Education" or "Exceptional Education" courses discussed the gifted child. Additionally, 75% of the institutions expressed interest in expanding their course offerings to include one or more on the gifted child. The authors concluded that despite this expressed interest, "altogether the institutions responding offered only a limited amount of attention in preparing teachers to approach the immense needs of the gifted child" (p. 95).

What are Teachers' Attitudes Toward the Gifted?

Teachers with no special preparation or background were found by researchers to be uninterested in or even hostile toward the gifted student (Wiener, 1960; Josephina, 1961). On the other hand, teachers with experience working in special programs for, or doing inservice presentations about, the gifted tended to be more enthusiastic about them (Wiener, 1960; Justman, 1951). Both Thomas (1973) and Jacobs (1971) found that regular classroom teachers' attitudes were frequently negative and filled with misconceptions concerning giftedness. They further implied that these biased attitudes were forcing gifted students to modify their classroom behavior, hide their real talents, and imitate the "less bright, more normal" child.

Reasons for teacher education undergraduates electing a class on education of the gifted were surveyed by Lazar (1973) and Lazar and Demos (1975). Curiosity about the gifted and creative, personal interest, and need for more knowledge were identified as key reasons for university students selecting the courses. Lazar (1973) felt that his study pointed up the need for more course offerings on the gifted at the university level to train "the teacher who is capable of meeting student needs, interests, and highly individual intellectual abilities and potentials" (p. 278).

What are Characteristics Of Teachers of the Gifted?

Authorities generally agree that successful teachers of the gifted have the following personality characteristics:

— mature and experienced; self-confident
— highly intelligent
— avocational interests that are intellectual in nature
— high achievement needs; desire for intellectual growth
— favorable attitude toward gifted children
— systematic, imaginative, flexible, and creative
— sense of humor
— willingness to be a "facilitator" rather than a "director" of learning
— hard working; willing to devote extra time and effort to teaching
— wide background of general knowledge; specific areas of expertise (especially secondary teachers)
— belief in and understanding of individual differences.

(Davis, 1954; Mirman, 1964; Maker, 1975; Bishop, 1968; Abraham, 1958; Ward, 1961; Gowan & Demos, 1964; Torrance, 1963; Gowan & Bruch, 1971; Marland, 1971; Newland, 1976; Gold, 1976; Gear, 1979).

Even though these traits are seen as desirable for all teachers, they are repeatedly listed as *essential* for teachers of the gifted. Maker (1975) attempted to narrow the list and identified two absolute necessities for a successful teacher of the gifted: a high degree of intelligence and knowledge about subject matter being taught, and emotional maturity coupled with a strong self-concept. In his review, Gold (1976) identified the same two prerequisite characteristics (high-level ability and ego strength) and pointed out the direct relationship between them.

Much has been written concerning the skills and qualifications of good teachers in general and, in the past decade, about specific competencies for teachers of the gifted. Seeley (1979) conducted a national survey of teacher competencies needed for education of the gifted. In this study a questionnaire was sent to universities, principals, and teachers involved in gifted education. Of 21 choices, respondents placed the following five competencies as highest in importance:

(1) Higher Cognitive Teaching and Questioning
(2) Curriculum Modification Strategies
(3) Special Curriculum Development Strategies
(4) Diagnostic-Prescriptive Teaching Skills
(5) Student Counseling Strategies. (p. 10)

Seeley also found agreement among his respondents that teachers of the gifted should have a master's degree in the field, experience in the regular classroom, and a variety of special competencies for teaching gifted children.

What is the Nature of Training For Teachers of the Gifted?

"Students enrolled in gifted child education coursework need assurance that their training will be as qualitatively differentiated as the methodologies they are taught to use with gifted children" (Hershey, 1979, p. 13). Literature indicates that preparation programs for teachers of the gifted should expect not only the mastery of concepts, but also application to real situations and analysis, synthesis, and evaluation of current philosophical approaches (Feldhusen, 1973; Newland, 1962; Rice, 1970; Hershey, 1979; Waskin, 1979). In his description of teacher training programs, Schnur (1977) felt the programs should "reflect some features of prescription and some flexibility... some of pedagogy and some of content. Perhaps the real quest is to train the teacher of the gifted to become a true master teacher" (p. 9).

Preservice training options include both undergraduate and graduate level university-based education programs for teachers preparing for direct service with gifted children. Periodically, surveys have been conducted to determine which colleges and universities offer courses or degree programs in gifted education (Laird & Kowalski, 1972; Seeley, 1979; Guy, 1979). Results have shown constant change, with a steady increase of opportunities available for teachers, both in number of courses offered and number of institutions offering training (Maker, 1975). The trend has been to offer graduate rather than undergraduate degree programs, with some emphasis on knowledge of gifted for all certified teachers (Seeley, 1979; Maker, 1975). This practice has ensured a solid background of liberal arts education before offering specialization.

The Special Education Report ("Teacher Training for the Gifted and Talented is Essential," 1978) listed the areas generally covered in training programs for teachers of gifted and talented. These include:

1. Characteristics and identification of gifted and talented

2. Understanding of cognitive, affective, and psychomotor processes, higher level thought processes

3. Teaching strategies, learning environments matched to gifted/talented interests and styles

4. Program organization and operation
5. Program evaluation.

The *Report* also recommended knowledge of research and its application to the classroom, and the ability to demonstrate teaching techniques and ideas.

What are the Current Trends in Training?

During 1981 Seeley and Hultgren (1982) conducted a study of teacher competencies and training. The primary purpose of this research was to determine the competencies or skill areas essential for teachers of gifted children. The secondary purpose was to determine to what extent university course offerings and pre- and inservice training programs have prepared practitioners, currently active in the field of gifted education, in the recognized competency areas.

Higher education programs for teachers/administrators of gifted programs existed in at least 140 colleges and universities in more than 40 states. The types of program options varied from one or two courses through entire degree programs at the master's, specialist, and doctoral levels. Most common was the master's program. Many responding universities indicated that their offerings were presently being expanded to include degree programs to meet certification standards. The number and types of professional programs in gifted education appeared to be on the increase at the time of this study.

A large sample of practitioners (N = 528) representing 48 states provided information. Teachers of the gifted, administrators in gifted programs, and a variety of instructional, curriculum, and support personnel were represented. The most common training options for teachers were inservice and staff development classes, and summer or workshop courses. Half the sample practitioner group (primarily the administrators and support personnel) held graduate degrees in education with emphasis on gifted. On the whole, the group was experienced, primarily coming from the regular or special education classroom, and seemed to be adequately prepared to teach in gifted programs. The practitioners rated competencies for teachers of the gifted as follows:

1. Knowledge of nature and needs of gifted
2. Skill in promoting higher cognitive thinking abilities and questioning techniques
3. Ability to develop methods and materials for the gifted
4. Knowledge of affective/psychological needs of the gifted
5. Skill in facilitating independent research and study skills
6. Ability to develop creative problem solving
7. Skill in individualizing teaching techniques
8. Knowledge of approaches to extension and enrichment of subject areas
9. Supervised practical experience teaching a group of gifted students.

What Training Should Be Required Of All Teachers?

The Seeley and Hultgren research indicated that more than three-fourths of both university program directors and practitioners in gifted education believed all professionally trained and certified teachers should have exposure to education of the gifted. Respondents preferred a separate semester or quarter course addressing topics in gifted education, for all teachers, rather than a shorter unit within general education coursework, as is currently the more common practice. Hesitation on the part of some universities might reflect problems involved in adopting new curriculum requirements for existing programs or perhaps the desire to isolate gifted education as a separate program or graduate level concentration.

With the current attention being focused on gifted education, an introductory course addressing the major competency areas would seem desirable for all teachers. Practitioners were highly in favor of this concept, perhaps because a majority had first been classroom teachers themselves. Practitioners realized that unless full-time special programs exist for gifted students, regular classroom teachers must assume a great responsibility for the affective and cognitive needs of gifted students. When programs do exist, teachers outside the gifted classroom greatly benefit from increased understanding of identification procedures and special strategies for gifted students.

What Changes are Needed in Training?

Institutions of higher education should offer a variety of quality program options to prepare teachers of the gifted. These programs should be taught by qualified faculty members and should address as many of the recognized competency areas as possible. Graduate degree programs with a variety of delivery systems are most appropriate. For institutions with established programs, new areas should be emphasized, including counseling, leadership training, cultural differences, current research, underachievers, parent/community relations, and educational technological developments. Universities must design programs for teachers of the gifted that are competency-based and sensitive to changing needs of the profession.

To ensure quality programs and professional security, practitioners working in gifted education should seek and demand high-level training. They should have available to them credit courses, degree programs, or inservice options based on relevant needs and competencies. Practitioners should continue to express concern about areas of training they deem important that have not been adequately covered in education programs. Program administrators should expect that new personnel would be of high caliber, would most likely be experienced teachers, and certainly should be especially trained to work with gifted students.

The competencies listed in the literature should be recognized as a minimal level of skill or knowledge to be required of teachers of gifted students. These lists of competencies, in addition to personal characteristics and experiences, might be used to evaluate prospective teachers according to specific program needs.

PARENTS AS FACILITATORS

What are the Characteristics Of Parents of the Gifted?

Goertzels and Goertzels (1962) reported a number of characteristics of parents of eminent people in their work. This retrospective study revealed the following characteristics of families:

— tended to be small families
— usually high socioeconomic status
— were Caucasian and lived in an urban area
— parents were professional
— family roots were English, German, Jewish, and Oriental
— often troubled homes with interpersonal conflicts.

The parents of the eminent people:

— placed high value on education and learning (not necessarily schooling)
— fostered an enjoyment for learning
— provided recognition and respect for their child's ability
— held strong opinions on social issues
— had little tolerance for rebellion in their child
— were dominating (mother or father)
— held negative attitudes toward school and teachers.

One must review these characteristics with some caution. The subjects of these studies were a small representation of gifted persons. The vast majority of gifted children we see in schools will never achieve the same level of national or international eminence as those reported by the Goertzels. This is not to diminish their potential contributions to society but, rather, to indicate the limited generalizability of family characteristics of eminent persons.

General themes concerning parents as reported elsewhere in the literature tend to both support and contradict the Goertzels' work. Some of the common themes were: (1) high degree of respect for the fathers who were professionals, (2) parents' sincere love of learning, and (3) stability of marriages (Roe, 1952; Terman, 1954).

Some evidence suggests that parents of gifted children are "pushy," both with their children and with schools. This, of course, tends to be in the "eye of the beholder." Parents of gifted children have high expectations and model high energy levels for learning and success in their own careers. Many educators view this image of the driving parent as detrimental to the development of gifted children. The previously cited research, however, supports this "push" as beneficial to the internal motivation of eminent persons. The paradox will perhaps always be with us in considering gifted children and their parents.

In recent research by Bloom and Sosniak (1981), parents were found to have a great influence on talent development of young eminent persons. They studied 120 persons who had distinguished themselves in three general areas: artistic talent, psychomotor talent, and cognitive talent. The groups included pianists and sculptors, Olympic swimmers and tennis players, and research mathematicians and research neurologists. Those authors reported common findings for the home and parenting styles of the majority of their subjects. These findings were that (1) a parent or relative had a personal interest in the child's talent area, (2) parents provided a model in valuing the talent, (3) parents encouraged and rewarded development of the talent through home activities, (4) parents "assumed that the children would wish to learn the talent emphasized by the parents" (pp. 87-88).

These results tend to support the previously cited research of parents of eminent people. No aversive or negative influences, however, were reported in the research. The notion of the pushy, driving parent was seen in a positive light relative to the realization of potential in the child.

How Should Parents
Relate to Schooling?

One of the greatest myths in education is that "all parents think their child is gifted." Parents are often so intimidated by this myth that they are compelled to amass large amounts of evidence of precocity just to begin discussion of schooling for their child. Some parents seek formal psychoeducational testing privately to confront schools for appropriate programming. Others provide information from home activities to demonstrate high abilities. The 6-year-old who routinely completes crossword puzzles in the *New York Times* and the 10-year-old who designs a laser machine to produce holographs are but two examples of children's home activities that parents have reported.

Schooling is often a frustrating experience for parents and their gifted children. Bloom and Sosniak (1981) nicely differentiate "schooling" from "talent development." They describe schooling as "...highly formalized, even in the early grades. There are written guidelines for what is to be learned and when it is to be learned...each individual is instructed as a member of a group with some notion that all are to get as nearly equal treatment as the teacher and the instructional material can supply" (p. 88). Talent development, however, is seen as instruction that is usually on a one-to-one basis with the instructor, who individually sets standards and timelines for mastery. "In talent development, each child was seen as unique...and there was continual adjustment to the child learning the talent" (p. 89).

Parents expect schools to provide "talent development," but their children usually get "schooling." Some schools come closer than others in individualizing instruction. Some have special programs for the gifted. But rarely do we find intensity of instruction in talent development when we look to schools. With varying degrees of success, parents have advocated and must continue to advocate for accommodations for their children. Public schools have the best resources to do the job. Mobilizing these resources is the greatest challenge we face in educating the gifted.

What should Schools Be Doing with Parents?

Parents can be either a formidable threat to teachers and administrators or productive partners in an evolution of schools. Schools should educate parents, but they also should be open to being educated by parents. This education must provide a process for change that is evolutionary, not revolutionary. Schools can enlist parents' support through active involvement rather than passive paternalism. Parents can approach schools in a helping rather than demanding way.

Delp and Martinson (1977) have offered some excellent suggestions for schools to involve parents. Some of their ideas are:

- Ask parents to provide information about their child to help determine interests, abilities, needs, and development.
- Have parents assist the teacher in organizing individual projects, mentorships, special interest groups, and field trips.
- Ask parents to serve on advisory committees to the school or district in creating and monitoring programs for the gifted.

These are just a few ideas for creating a climate in which parents can participate in the evolution. We as educators must listen to parents and seek their support if we are to have a significant impact on the child's potential.

SUPPORT PERSONNEL AS FACILITATORS

What is the Role of Psychologists?

Psychologists can play a key role in identifying gifted children and in counseling them and their parents. Unfortunately, many psychologists receive little if any training related to the gifted. Psychologists are usually exposed to the medical model of looking for deficits through testing. Often they learn about gifted children on the job, and many become quite adept at examining children for strengths and special abilities. The deficit orientation of psychologists has to be overcome through training and experience. The emergence of more school programs for the gifted has necessitated new assignments and new approaches for psychologists. We are now seeing some changes that may be adopted for preservice and inservice training of psychologists.

Psychologists have good skills in intellectual assessment for their professional activity. Their expertise in this area is important to the testing and identification of giftedness. The intellectual assessment, coupled with good individual achievement testing, should culminate in a clear direction for parents and educators. This direction is usually a series of recommendations based on both strengths and needs identified.

Psychologists can also serve an important role in counseling parents and gifted children themselves. Their knowledge of development, learning theory, and interpersonal dynamics can assist in understanding both the intellectual and personality characteristics of gifted children. Precocious behaviors on one hand and normal developmental growth on the other constitute a delicate balance. Psychologists should inform parents, educators, and children about coping with this balance in the most productive ways.

As we learn more through research and experience with gifted learners, psychologists must be involved—not only in inputting information to this knowledge base but also in translating it into improved assessment and programming. Understanding the uniqueness of gifted children as well as the implications for their normal development are important concepts involving psychologists.

What is the Role
Of School Counselors?

Alexander and Muia (1982) have described the special role of school counselors in stating, "...exceptionally bright learners, plagued at times by concomitant problems associated with their giftedness, require the warmth, support, and understanding of competent, caring persons—a job description suited to the school's guidance and counseling personnel" (p. 173). Counselors can provide a unique service in facilitating the growth of gifted students in the school context. Counselors are usually familiar with the academic programming and resources of the school. They can work closely with other support personnel in carrying out recommendations of the psychologist in the important planning function for the gifted child's academic and social life.

Counselors must be sensitive to the unique needs of the gifted in order to become "environmental engineers." Scheduling appropriate classes, matching student needs with teacher styles, and counseling parents are but a few key roles counselors serve in creating a growth environment. They must also be concerned with the long-term implications of educational and career planning. This is indeed a complex task for these busy professionals. Counselors are often burdened with heavy caseloads, necessitating special approaches to organizing services to special populations of learners such as the gifted.

Realizing the limitations of time, counselors must marshal all the help they can get from a variety of resources. Some approaches counselors use to extend their services include:

1. Setting up a teacher-advisor program for gifted students, in which a key teacher the student likes, who teaches in an area of interest of the student, serves as the advisor for planning courses, activities, and perhaps mentorships.

2. Organizing groups for the gifted, wherein these students come together periodically to discuss problems and share experiences concerning the academic and social life of the school.

3. Establishing a career education resource center so that gifted students can explore careers through guided reading and can identify appropriate community mentors for visitations.

4. Providing a special information file for the gifted to explain programs such as Advanced Placement, CLEP exams, National Merit Scholarships, universities' honor programs, and so on.

5. Organizing gifted students to create a "survival package" for new gifted students entering the school, which gives insights into "good" teachers, special access to labs and computers, special clubs and extracurricular activities, and names and phone numbers of other gifted students available as personal resources.

All of these things can help counselors extend their services through self-directed, peer-directed, and teacher-directed activities. The organizing will take time, but once the processes are in place, the investment should pay off.

Counselors are needed at all levels to be advocates and "educational engineers" for the gifted. Unfortunately, their services are usually restricted to the secondary level. Schools that have elementary counselors are in a good position to utilize vertical planning for gifted students. The counselor's role is an important one for all schools to utilize in programming for the gifted. The challenge lies in mobilizing these resources productively.

MENTORS AS FACILITATORS

Who are Mentors for the Gifted?

Anyone can be a mentor to a gifted child. Teachers and parents are constantly surprised at whom the child will identify as a mentor. In a general sense, a mentor is a person the child admires, who provides a role model in some area of human endeavor and who serves both to stimulate and respect the child. The role varies from hero to colleague but always implies admiration and respect.

From the school's standpoint, mentors for gifted children are usually identified for them by teachers who wish to extend classroom instruction using key individuals in the community. This assignment of child to community resource person assumes a mentor relationship. If we keep the above definition in mind, however, this does not always meet the child's standards for a mentor. The term is used loosely in gifted education. We should think of two dimensions of the term. In the jargon of gifted education, a mentor is a resource person, usually from the community, who can provide supplemental educational experiences in some area of expertise. This person may be a computer analyst, an artist, or an urban geographer. Whether the child perceives this person as a mentor is subject to individual interpretation, but rarely does a community resource person become a true mentor for the child.

We in gifted education must explain the full range of mentor relationships to gifted children. They should understand that a community resource person may be called a mentor for program purposes but that the child has other significant, personal mentors—parent, relative, neighbor, teacher, or other.

The role of mentors in development of eminent persons has been significant. Research on adult development also stresses the importance of mentors in personal and career success (Goertels & Goertzels, 1962; Levinson, Darrow, Klein, Levinson, & McKee, 1978). Levinson has pointed out not only the need to have mentors but also the need to understand the amount and kind of mentoring.

What are the Roles of Mentors?

The role of mentor as discussed here will follow the reasoning set forth. The personal mentor could be anyone the gifted student identifies as having a major influence. The resource person is someone a school program might identify to work with a gifted student.

The Personal Mentor

Levinson et al. (1978) have provided excellent insights into the role of the personal mentor. The mentor may be a *teacher* who enhances the student's skills and intellectual development. A mentor may be a *sponsor* using influence to facilitate the child's advancement. A mentor may be a *host and guide* into a new world, acquainting the student with values, customs, and resources. "Through his own virtues, achievements, and way of living, the mentor may be an *exemplar* that the protégé can admire and seek to emulate. He may provide *counsel* and moral support in time of stress" (p. 98).

They also discussed the outcomes of the mentor relationship, stating that the student "...may take the admired qualities of the mentor more fully into himself. He may become better able to learn from himself, to listen to the voices from within. His personality is enriched as he makes the mentor a more intrinsic part of himself. The internalization of significant figures is a major source of development in adulthood" (p. 101). Although those authors were discussing the mentor relationship as applied to the development of young men, they do give us an excellent paradigm for application to all precocious youth.

The Resource Mentor

School programs may assign mentors to supplement gifted children's education. They are usually volunteers from the community who invite gifted children to visit their places of work. Boston (1976) has nicely defined this role as "...the anchoring of the pupil's learning in experience and the mentor's use of the pupil's predilection" (p. 2). Boston (1978) noted the importance of matching not only the interest of the child to the expertise of the mentor, but also matching the teaching style to the learning style. He described the important characteristics of the mentor as follows:

1. Usually, but not always an adult

2. Has a special skill, interest, or activity that engages the learner's interest

3. Is able to guide the learner toward personally rewarding experiences

4. Is flexible, helping the learner review and revise activities

5. Is often a role model for the learner. The mentor can impart an understanding of life style and attitudes different from those the student might ordinarily meet

6. Is above all interested in the student as a learner and as an individual. (p. 1)

These characteristics and roles must be addressed in finding appropriate community mentors for the gifted. Mentorships, both personal and school-based, are essential to fully developing talent and abilities in gifted children.

SUMMARY

Teachers, parents, support personnel, and mentors are all critical ingredients in the development of the whole child. Development of this talent pool is essential to the future of our society. We must continue to educate and expand the cadre of facilitators if we are to realize the contributions of these talented young people.

This chapter by no means represents an exhaustive review of facilitators who might impact the life of a gifted child. As indicated at the outset of this chapter, the possibilities of significant people are many, including but not limited to those discussed here. Grandparents, siblings, friends, and school principals are just a few others who might be important facilitators.

The roles and relationships of facilitators to gifted children must be seen as a collective network that changes over time. In educating gifted children, we must recognize and utilize this network of facilitators in fulfilling our mission.

REFERENCES

Abraham, W. *Common sense about gifted children.* New York: Harper & Bros., 1958.

Alexander, P., & Muia, J. *Gifted education.* Rockville, MD: Aspen Systems Corp., 1982.

Bishop, W.E. Successful teachers of the gifted. *Exceptional Children,* 1968, *34,* 317-325.

Bloom, B.S., & Sosniak, L. Talent development versus schooling. *Educational Leadership,* 1981, *39,* 85-94.

Boston, B.O. *The sorcerer's apprentice.* Reston, VA: ERIC Clearinghouse on Handicapped and Gifted Children, 1975.

Boston, B.O. *Developing a community based mentorship program for gifted and talented.* Washington, DC: Office of Gifted and Talented, U.S. Department of Health, Education and Welfare, 1978.

Davis, N. Teachers of the gifted. *Journal of Teacher Education,* 1954, *5,* 221-224.

Delp, J.L., & Martinson, R.A. *The gifted and talented: A handbook for parents.* Ventura, CA: County Superintendent of Schools, 1975.

Feldhusen, J. Practicum activities for students and gifted children in a university course. *Gifted Child Quarterly,* 1973, *17,* 124-129.

Gallagher, J. *Analysis of research on the education of gifted children.* Springfield, IL: Office of Superintendent of Public Instruction, 1960.

Gardner, J. *Excellence: Can we be equal and excellent too?* New York: Harper & Row, 1961.

Gear, G. Teachers of the gifted; a student's perspective. *Roeper Review,* 1979, *1,* 18-20.

Goertzels, V., & Goertzels, M. *Cradles of eminence.* Boston: Little, Brown, 1962.

Gold, M. Preparation of teachers for gifted and talented youngsters. *Talents and Gifts,* 1976, *19,* 22-23.

Gowan, J., & Bruch, C. What makes a creative person a creative teacher? In J. Gowan & P. Torrance (Eds.), *Educating the ablest.* Itasca, IL: F.E. Peacock, Publishers, 1971, 165-169.

Gowan, J., & Demos, G.D. *The education of the ablest.* Springfield, IL: Charles C Thomas, 1964.

Guy, M.E. *Introductory education for teachers of gifted children in the United States.* Paper presented to 3rd International Conference on Gifted/Talented Children, Jerusalem, July 1979.

Hershey, M. Toward a theory of teacher education for the gifted and talented. *Roeper Review,* 1979, *1,* 12-14.

Jacobs, J.C. Teacher attitude toward gifted children. *Gifted Child Quarterly,* 1972, *16,* 23-26.

Justman, J. Obstacles to the improvement of teaching in classes for the gifted. *Exceptional Children,* 1951, *18,* 41-45.

Laird, A.W., & Kowalski, C.J. Survey of 1,564 colleges and universities on courses offered in the education of the gifted—Teacher training. *Gifted Child Quarterly,* 1972, *16,* 93-111.

Lazar, A. Reasons cited by college students in teacher training for taking an elective course on education of the gifted. *Gifted Child Quarterly,* 1973, *17,* 274-278.

Lazar, A., & Demos, G. *Reasons for taking a course about the gifted.* Long Beach: California State University, Oct. 1975. (ERIC Document Reproduction Service No. ED 136504)

Levinson, D., Darrow, C.N., Klein, E.B., Levinson, M.H., & McKee, B. *Seasons of a man's life.* New York: Alfred A. Knopf,1978.

Maker, C.J. *Training teachers for the gifted and talented: A comparison of models.* Reston, VA: Council for Exceptional Children, 1975.

Marland, S.P. *Education of the gifted and talented* (Vol. 2). Washington, DC: U.S. Office of Education, 1971.

Mirman, N. Teacher qualifications for educating the gifted. *Gifted Child Quarterly,* 1964, *8,* 123-126.

Newland, T.E. Some observations on essential qualifications of teachers of the mentally superior. *Exceptional Children,* 1962, *29,* 111-114.

Newland, T.E. The gifted in socio-educational perspective. Englewood Cliffs, NJ: Prentice-Hall, 1976.

Piaget, J. Piaget's theory. In P.H. Mussen (Ed.), *Carmichael's manual of child psychology* (3rd ed.) (2 vols.). New York: Wiley, 1970.

Rice, J. *The gifted: Developing total talent.* Springfield, IL: Charles C Thomas, 1970.

Roe, A. *The making of a scientist.* New York: Dodd, Mead, 1952.

Schnur, J. *Description of a teacher training program for the education of the gifted.* Paper presented at the 5th Annual Conference on Gifted and Talented Education, Ames, IA, Oct. 1977.

Seeley, K.R. Competencies for teachers of gifted and talented children. *Journal for the Education of the Gifted,* 1979, *3,* 7-13.

Seeley, K.R., & Hultgren, H. *Training teachers of the gifted* (Research monograph). Denver: University of Denver, 1982.

Snider, G. Preservice and inservice education for teachers of the gifted. In B. Shertzer (Ed.), *Working with superior students.* Chicago: Science Research Associates, 1960, pp. 269-278.

Tannenbaum, A. Pre-Sputnik to post-Watergate concern about the gifted. In A.H. Passow (Ed.), *The gifted and talented: Their education and development* (78th yearbook of the National Society for the Study of Education, Part 1). Chicago: University of Chicago Press, 1979.

Teacher training for the gifted and talented is essential. *Special Education Report,* 1978, *529,* 1-3.

Terman, L.M. The discovery and encouragement of exceptional talent. *American Psychologist,* 1954, *9,* 221-230.

Thomas, S.B. Neglecting the gifted causes them to hide their talents. *Gifted Child Quarterly,* 1973, *17,* 193-197.

Torrance, E.P. *Guiding creative talent.* Englewood Cliffs, NJ: Prentice-Hall, 1963.

Ward, V. *Educating the gifted: An axiomatic approach.* Columbus, OH: Charles E. Merrill, 1961.

Waskin, Y. Filling the gap. *Roeper Review,* 1979, *1,* 9-11.

Wiener, J. A study of the relationship between selected variables and attitudes of teachers toward gifted children (Doctoral dissertation, University of California at Los Angeles, 1960). *American Doctoral Dissertations,* 1960, *54.*

Wilson, F.T. Preparation for teachers of gifted children. *Exceptional Children,* 1953, *20,* 78-80.

Wilson, F. The preparation of teachers for the education of gifted children. In R. Havighurst (Ed.), *Education for the gifted* (57th yearbook of the National Society for the Study of Education, Part 2). Chicago: University of Chicago Press, 1958.

ADDITIONAL REFERENCES

Aubrecht, L. *Response to the task force recommendations concerning the development of educational leadership.* Paper presented to National Forum on Minority Disadvantaged Gifted and Talented, Washington, DC, May 1978.

Breiter, J. *Survey: Teachers of gifted elementary students.* Ames, IA: Iowa State University of Science and Technology, 1979. (ERIC Document Reproduction Service No. ED 170987)

Bruch, C. Current degree programs in gifted education. *Gifted Child Quarterly,* 1977, *21,* 142-153.

Bruch, C. Missing qualities in training educators for the gifted and talented. *Gifted Child Quarterly,* 1977, *21,* 137-141.

Buttery, T.J. Preservice teachers' attitude regarding gifted children. *College Student Journal,* 1978, *12,* 288-289.

Clark, B. *Growing up gifted: Developing the potential of children at home and at school.* Columbus, OH: Charles E. Merrill, 1979.

Cohn, S.J. Changing teachers' attitudes and behaviors toward the gifted student. *Talents and Gifts,* 1977, *19,* 23-26.

Competency-based programs for certification—Gifted and talented. Raleigh, NC: State Department of Public Instruction, 1976.

Correll, M. *Teaching the gifted and talented* (Fastback 119). Bloomington, IN: Phi Delta Kappa, 1978. (ERIC Document Reproduction Service No. ED 166 887)

Curry, J., & Sato, I. Training on the right track. *Gifted Child Quarterly,* 1977, *21,* 200-204.

Feldhusen, J. Meeting the needs of gifted children and teachers in a university course. *Gifted Child Quarterly,* 1977, *21,* 195-200.

Fox, L. The values of gifted youths. In D.P. Keating (Ed.), *Intellectual talent: Research and development.* Baltimore: Johns Hopkins University Press, 1976, 273-284.

Fraiser, M. The third dimension. *Gifted Child Quarterly,* 1977, *21,* 207-213.

Gallagher, J., & Weiss, P. *The education of gifted and talented students: A history and prospectus.* Washington, DC: Council for Basic Education, 1979.

George, W.C. Discussion of barriers to education of the gifted. *Talents and Gifts,* 1977, *19,* 2-4.

Gold, H. Training teachers for the gifted. *Gifted Child Quarterly,* 1963, *7,* 93-97.

Gold, M. Teachers and mentors. In A. H. Passow (Ed.), *The gifted and talented: Their education and development* (78th yearbook of the National Society for the Study of Education, Part 1). Chicago: University of Chicago Press, 1979.

Guy, M.E. What gifted education texts do colleges use? *Journal for the Education of the Gifted,* 1979, *2,* 94-98.

Hauck, B., & Freehill, M. *The gifted—Case studies.* Dubuque, IA: William C. Brown Co., 1972.

Hershey, M., & Hall, H. Summer programs for the gifted: Keys to future teacher training? *Journal for the Education of the Gifted,* 1978, *1,* 38-43.

Hultgren, H. *Competencies for teahcers of the gifted.* Doctoral dissertation, University of Denver, 1981.

Issacs, A. A survey of suggested preparation for teachers of the gifted. *Gifted Child Quarterly,* 1966, *10,* 72-77.

Jacobs, J.C. Effectiveness of teacher and parent identification of gifted children as a function of school level. *Psychology in the Schools,* 1971, *8,* 140-142.

Josephina, Sister. Teachers' reactions to gifted children. *Gifted Child Quarterly,* 1961, *5,* 42-44.

Kaplan, S. *Providing programs for the gifted and talented: A handbook.* Ventura, CA: National Summer Leadership Training Institute on the Education of the Gifted and Talented, June 1974.

Karnes, F., & Collins, E. Teacher certification in gifted education: A national survey. *Gifted Child Quarterly,* 1977, *21,* 204-207.

Lindsey, M. *Training teachers of the gifted and talented.* New York: Teachers College, Columbia University, 1980.

Lyon, H.C. The federal perspective on gifted and talented. *Journal for the Education of the Gifted,* 1980, *4,* 3-7.

Maker, C.J. *Providing programs for the gifted handicapped.* Reston, VA: Council for Exceptional Children, 1977.

Martinson, R.A. *The identification of the gifted and talented.* Ventura, CA: Office of Ventura County Superintendent of Schools, 1974.

Martinson, R.A *A guide toward better teaching for the gifted.* Los Angeles: National/State Leadership Training Institute, 1976.

McCarthy, R. *Assessment of competencies of teachers of the intellectually gifted.* Nassau County, NY: Agate Press, Oct. 1979.

Mitchell, B. What's happening to gifted education in the United States today? *Phi Delta Kappan,* 1980, *61,* 563-564.

Mohan, M. Is there a need for a course in creativity in teacher education? *Journal of Creative Behavior,* 1973, *7,* 175-186.

Passow, A.H. Styles of leadership training. *G/C/T,* 1978, *1,* 9-12.

Pegnato, C.W., & Birch, J.W. Locating gifted children in junior high schools: A comparison of methods. *Exceptional Children,* 1959, *25,* 300-304.

Plowman, P. Training teachers. *Roeper Review,* 1979, *1,* 14-17.

Renzulli, J. Identifying key features in programs for the gifted. *Exceptional Children,* 1968, *35,* 217-221.

Renzulli, J. Instructional management systems: A model for organizing and developing inservice training workshops. *Gifted Child Quarterly,* 1977, *21,* 186-187.

Rogers, P. On being a successful teacher of the gifted. *Gifted Child Quarterly,* 1965, *9,* 194-201.

Rosen, J. *Perceptions of the childhood self and teacher-child relations.* New York: Bank Street College of Education, 1975. (ERIC Document Reproduction Service No. ED 115 604)

Sandberg, J.H. Teachers for the gifted: Mandates. In *Selected convention papers, 1963—Council for Exceptional Children convention.* Arlington, VA: Council for Exceptional Children, 1963.

Sato, I., & Johnson, B. Multifaceted training meets multidimensionally gifted. *Journal of Creative Behavior,* 1978, *12,* 63-71.

Shaffer, V., & Troutt, G. Courses offered on the education of the gifted. *Gifted Child Quarterly,* 1970, *14,* 8-23.

Silverman, L.K. *How are gifted teachers different from other teachers?* Paper presented at National Association for Gifted Children Conference, Minneapolis, Oct. 1980.

Sisk, D. Teaching the gifted and talented teacher: A training model. *Gifted Child Quarterly,* 1975, *19,* 81-88.

Sisk, D. Education of the gifted and talented: A national perspective. *Journal for the Education of the Gifted,* 1978, *1,* 5-24.

Sisk, D. Issues and future directions in gifted education. *Gifted Child Quarterly,* 1980, *24,* 29-32.

Skipper, C. Intellectually gifted people and their potential as teachers. *Kappa Delta Pi Record,* 1974, *10,* 83-87.

Solano, C. Teacher and pupil stereotypes of gifted boys and girls. *Talents and Gifts,* 1977, *19,* 4-8.

Speed, F. Teaching the bright child. *Orbit 41,* 1978, *9,* 6-11.

Syphers, D.F. *Gifted and talented children: Practical programming for teachers and principals.* Arlington, VA: Council for Exceptional Children, 1972.

Tompkins, J., & Stahl, R. Teacher preparation for the gifted child. *North Carolina Association for the Gifted and Talented Quarterly Journal,* 1976, *2,* 24-29.

VanTassel, J. TAG presidential address, Philadelphia, 1980. *Journal for the Education of the Gifted,* 1980, *3.*

Wilson, F. Teacher education and the gifted. *Journal of Teacher Education,* 1955, *6,* 236-267.

Witters, L. The needs of rural teachers in gifted education. *Journal for the Education of the Gifted,* 1980, *3,* 79-81.

Zettel, J. State provisions for educating the gifted and talented. In A.H. Passow (Ed.), *The gifted and talented: Their education and development* (78th yearbook of the National Society for the Study of Education, Part 1). Chicago: University of Chicago Press, 1979.

Zettel, J., & Ballard, J. A need for increased federal effort for the gifted and talented. *Exceptional Children,* 1978, *44,* 261-267.

Helping a Child toward Individual Excellence

William Foster

"Everything that liberates our minds without giving us control over ourselves is ruinous." To those working for the successful development of gifted children, these words of Johann Wolfgang von Goethe hold much import. They speak to us from the

135

19th century, reminding us of the importance of balancing liberty with control. The special freedom bestowed on an individual as a consequence of his or her exceptional ability should not be allowed to run rampant in the person or in society, producing an "enfant terrible." This liberty must be complemented by the emergence of a mature pattern of personality and behavior that helps the individual act on his or her talent in a personally meaningful but socially responsible fashion.

Goethe's injunction serves as a kind of warning to us not to leave this process to chance in the hope that serendipity will intervene, making all things turn out good. Serendipity is too fickle. Transforming an individual's exceptional potential into a mature expression of originality and productivity is an arduous task—long, complex, and planful. Even when done conscientiously, the effort often falls short of what was originally hoped for. Such an arduous traverse must not be done alone. Good guidance and counsel are invaluable to the process, especially that part concerned with the evolution of an integrated and secure, yet flexible and socially competent personality—all important to the eventual realization of individual excellence (Foster, 1982).

PSYCHOSOCIAL DEVELOPMENT IN THE GIFTED

This psychosocial development of the precocious child has been of concern to many. Perhaps the most articulate has been Leta Hollingworth (1942). Her work is still a landmark of insight into the emotional and social aspects of growing up gifted. By now others have taken on the task of expanding our appreciation of the many factors involved in the successful transformation of an able child into a mature, productive adult (Silverman, 1982; Richert, 1983; Delisle, 1982; Colangelo & Zaffrann, 1979). The approach to psychosocial development most characteristic of these writers is based in the existential, humanistic traditions of 19th and 20th century philosophy and psychology. Directly or indirectly, their work pivots on ideas such as Sartre's call for an active engagement of the world in the search for a personal essence, and Maslow's notion of a self-actualizing tendency in each human being.

The Self-Actualizing Tendency

The dynamic of the self-actualizing tendency is often referred to as the "third" or "autonomous" factor of personality development. It is called the third factor because it stands in contrast to the other two factors traditionally assumed to explain personality development—biological inheritance and social environment. Either separately or in combination, these two factors, the one articulated through psychodynamic theory and the other through behaviorism, are widely assumed to be the cause of personality formation. Maslow (1968) and others (Rogers, 1954; Dambrowski, 1964; Fromm, 1947) proposed that neither of these, alone or together, is sufficient to explain the total of human development. So they offered this third factor of development, a component that allows for the transcendence of an individual beyond biological or environmental determinism to levels of self-actualization congruent with an integrated, creative personality.

Goethe, with the prescience of third factor psychology, declared, "stirli und merde," die and grow (Seidlin, 1982). In this phrase he captured a basic characteristic of the evolution of the person coincident with the effective transformation of a raw potential into an expressed, disciplined talent. This transforming is not simply a process of accretion, piling one block upon the next, but a metamorphosis from one stage of individual development to another. The transformations are not simply quantitative but are qualitative in character. Analogous to Piaget's (1960) model of cognitive, structural transformation, this view of personality development acknowledges that the disintegration (death) of one stage of development and the integration (growth) of a qualitatively distinct pattern of personality and behavior may be a painful struggle for the individual. Therefore, periods of personal anxiety and depression are not of themselves considered dysfunctional experiences but must be judged in the context of the person's overall life experience (Piechowski, 1983).

The Psychosocial Process

The particulars of the psychosocial process involved in this transformation are certainly multitudinous and, for the most part, remain speculative and obscure. The recent work of four scholars, Montour, Albert, Piechowski, and Bloom, however, provides a framework for building a fuller appreciation of the workings of this intensive and extensive process.

Montour's (1977) fine comparative case study of the early lives of William Sidis and Norbert Wiener gives us a perspective on the role of parents in the unfolding personality and behavior of the precocious child. Albert's (1980) analysis of numerous psychosocial and sociological variables, such as birth order and parental occupation, provides a hint of the array of familial and socioeconomic influences on the youngsters participating in the Johns Hopkins Precocious Math Project through intensive life history analyses of people like Saint-Exupéry and Eleanor Roosevelt. Piechowski (1983) and his collaborators have empirically linked the tendency toward self-actualization to certain fundamental theoretical constructs of personality development such as developmental potential and its concomitant set of psychic overexcitabilities. And Bloom and Sosniak's (1981) retrospective life analysis takes us beyond the realm of individual psychic sibling and family interactions to a consideration of extrafamilial variables such as teacher/mentor practices and the larger impact of social institutions including schools.

Part of what has been noted by these researchers serves as a confirmation of the earlier work of Hollingworth (1942) and Pressey (1955) on the psychosocial variables affecting the precocious child. We can look forward to more insights from Feldman's (1982) current longitudinal analysis of the day-to-day activities of six precocious youngsters at Tufts University. From works like this, we begin to appreciate some of the factors involved in the elaborate web of variables that make up the effective facilitation of excellence in individual lives.

The major thrust of this body of work has been and continues to be psychosocial in character; that is, the study of how the transformation of exceptional potential proceeds toward realized accomplishment is mainly focused upon the interpersonal, social-psychological, and sociological variables of the process. Piechowski's work is the major exception to this tendency;

he and his colleagues are studying psychological variables congruent with the third force proposition of self-actualization.

The discussion here, in its turn, deals primarily with the psychosocial aspects of how individual excellence may be achieved, focusing upon the planful interventions that constitute an organized approach to providing guidance and counsel during this long, arduous traverse. Like Piechowski, however, it assumes that a fundamental quality crucial to the successful realization of individual excellence is wholly psychological and organismic in character.

Fundamental Psychological Constructs

For purposes of this chapter, the psychological quality of exceptional ability is considered to be that descriptive characterization of an individual's potential at a relatively early period in his or her life. Expanding on Renzulli (1978), it is best understood to be the consequence of an overlap of four broad, yet fundamental psychological constructs, or domains—*ability, creativity, motivation,* and *self-concept.*

Excellence, on the other hand, is viewed as an outcome or a goal to be attained by the individual. This attainment is highly dependent upon a favorable mix of psychosocial factors in an individual's life and cannot be assumed to be the inevitable fruition of early potential. Specifically, excellence is an evaluative statement about a person's behavior later in life and relates to his or her level of originality and productivity in some self-selected domain of performance.

The Process of Transformation

As parents, educators, and friends, the aim of our involvement in the life of a child must be to aid that child in transforming his or her potential into a mature pattern of personality and behavior conducive to the realization of individual excellence. To be of such assistance, we must have some road map of the transition. Our guidance and counsel must be aimed at a set of goals integral to successful adulthood. The task at hand is like that of turning static energy into a kinetic form, promise to fulfillment. Figure 6 portrays such a road map, such a heuristic.

Like all road maps, this one's utility is in relation to its distinction. Giftedness as a construct finds its full utility in relation to later life goals such as productivity and individual excellence. "The construct of excellence allows for a focus on works rather than promise. It is an open-ended rather than a deterministic notion. It suggests the positive aspects of merit as a social yardstick.... It is something educators can sponsor in stu-

---

FIGURE 6
Transformation Toward Excellence

initial characteristics of the gifted individual	intermediate characteristics of the same individual upon entrance to school
• rich developmental potential	• high ability
• an active curiosity	• above average creativity
• high energy level	• consistent motivation
• extended perceptual field	• emerging self-concept

cluster of these same characteristics
in the mature, innovative person
• a specific body of knowledge, skill, process, and value appropriate to a chosen career or occupation
• a consistent pattern of acting in original and productive ways
• an orientation to hard work and persistence at a specific task
• an integrated, secure yet evolving sense of self that effectively mediates between the individual's unique view of the world and the more socially typical view of that same world

dents, something they can insist on. With it no one is a fortunate, though passive recipient of 'the gift'" (Foster, 1982).

At least two sets of psychosocial factors serve as catalysts in the successful realization of this destination:

intimate associates	*social institutions*
• parents	• the general cultural milieu
• family members	• planned learning environments including schools
• teachers/mentors	
• friends	• work places

This transformation is a developmentally sensitive learning process in which the child's native capacity blends with the lessons he or she learns from intimate associates and social institutions during his or her life. The subtle evolution hopefully results in a mature pattern of personality and behavior suited to the pursuit of individual excellence. This learning occurs in at least three distinct ways—through modeling, through social injunction, and through technical instruction (Hall, 1973).

Through modeling, each of us learns deeply embedded lessons of living. The essence of this process is perhaps best expressed by transposing the old saw to: "Do as I do, not as I say." Youngsters incorporate a value for reading because they see their intimates reading, and posture the event even before they know which end of the book is up.

Through social injunction, they learn the cultural folkways and mores of their immediates. They are told by the incantation of ritualized injunction that girls do not do mathematics. "Sugar and spice and everything nice; that's what little girls are made of" while "snakes and snails and puppy dog tails; that's what little boys are made of" direct young lives in gentle yet powerful ways.

Last, through technical instruction children begin to learn the overt curriculum of life. This curriculum ranges from how to tie a shoe to how to conjugate a Latin verb.

From the earliest moments of awareness, the child is constantly experiencing each of these patterns of learning. To appreciate the continual impact, however covert, of modeling and social injunction upon mature life experience is vital. Often, in spite of the overt technical learnings, these two forms of knowing take precedence, as in the aforementioned tendency of mathematically precocious girls to move away from mathematical careers (Fox, 1976) or of able females to describe themselves in the sugar-and-spice images of learned helplessness (Dweck, 1975).

Much of the individual's psychosocial learning occurs on this covert level. The curriculum of psychosocial transformations toward excellence is usually left to the unfocused whims of such inarticulate learning. Serendipity is little match for such implicit and implacable forces. Helping a child toward those psychosocial leanings conducive to individual excellence has to be a thoughtful, organized process of guidance and counsel.

Psychosocial Needs of the Gifted Child

Gowan (1977) has made clear the special psychosocial needs of the gifted child. He and others (Perrone & Male, 1981) have developed elaborate lists of special issues for our attention. Among these, four basic observations stand out. These represent general issues for attention in developing an overt, technical curriculum to complement the usual covert psychosocial development of the individual child.

Inherent tension is present between the unusual expectations and needs of the gifted child and the normative standards of the larger society. Often, a clear discontinuity of experience and expectation exists between what an able child is ready to do and what he or she is expected and allowed to do. The personal ambiguity generated by having one's experience of reality be distinct from the norm creates tension in the emotional life of the individual, a tension that is often resolved by surrendering one's difference for the relative peace and anonymity of being normal. Rather than opting out of this tension, the gifted person must be taught to effectively manage that tension throughout his or her life.

The child may be aware of developmentally relevant tasks prior to his or her having the resources with which to resolve them. The idea of intellectual or performance acceleration is a well-established proposition for those working with able young-sters. Less appreciated is the possibility of similar acceleration in the affective or social domain.

The experience of one 7-year-old girl highlights this circumstance. One evening at bedtime she announced her intention to kill herself. Her parents were understandably distraught by this declaration and promptly told the girl not to talk of such things. This morbid proposition, however, became the focus of a series of going-to-bed discussions. As bedtime had traditionally been a time to talk over important concerns of the day, her statements could not be disregarded. What was this all about? Why did this very capable, likeable little girl persist in talking about self-destruction? Certainly the parents' denial of her concern was not wise. And their denial did not quell her one bit, as evidenced by her persistent voicing of her desire.

Using the idea of psychosocial acceleration as a basis for analyzing the situation provides a possible explanation. Erickson (1950) and others (Havighurst, 1953) have suggested that all of us proceed through a series of developmental tasks and that these tasks are chronological in character. During adolescence, the principle task to be accomplished is that of establishing a sense of identity. Complex in character, this task is perhaps best summarized as the process of answering questions such as, "Who am I, separate from my family and friends?"

One thing that receives much attention during this time is an engagement with the idea of death and nonbeing, for to understand the essentials of identity, individuals must grapple with the possibility of their nonexistence. Often during this difficult exploration of self, adolescents express ideations about death and suicide (just ask any high school English teacher about some of the topics of students' themes and stories). Unfortunately, much too often these symbolic considerations transform into action, making adolescence a high-risk time. Could the 7-year-old girl's consideration of suicide, an atypical concern for children of that age, possibly be a reflection of developmental acceleration?

In this case, the parents decided to behave as if it were, and began to engage her concern as legitimate, needing open, straightforward review. As talks proceeded, the girl reframed her concern to, "I wonder what it will be like when I die?"—certainly a powerful and healthy developmental question. Through continued discussions, some bedtime reading of selected books in which characters dealt with the same issue, and a lot of emotional support for the OK-ness of her concern, the child eventually turned to other issues and experiences as the subject of evening conversation. The developmental task of identity was certainly not resolved by these bedtime talks, but its initial consideration was well handled. Her parents had become effective resources for their daughter's development, accelerated as it was.

A similar yet somewhat contrary correlate to the idea of developmental acceleration proposes that children gain intellectual independence from their parents and immediate family before gaining their emotional or social independence. Exceptional intellectual capacity is the characteristic most frequently used to define the able child. Early reading, lots of puzzles and problem solving, constant questioning and reliable answering all begin to define a framework for the complementary exchange between parents and child. As time goes on, the gifted child's questions become ones that elders can not as easily answer, their books are now ones that the parents have not read, their problems are addressed to computers while the adults may remain computer illiterate. The framework that evolved for defining the parent-child relationship begins to come apart much sooner than usual and the roles reverse, with the child having more to offer than the parent.

Because the domain of the intellect has been so deeply and subtly embedded as the primary mechanism for carrying the relationship, parents and child both become bereft of a way of maintaining that helpful degree of dependence typical of later childhood and early adolescence. Support for the child's emotional and social needs can become problematic, creating a sense of isolation in both parents and child. To treat a gifted child as an adult in all things when he or she is still a child in most cases is just as wrong as to treat the child as a child in all things when he or she is an adult in some (Foster & Gatto, 1980).

Finally, the child needs more adequate role models. Remembering the central function that modeling plays in the psychosocial education of children, youngsters must have adults that model behaviors representative of mature, productive lives. Recalling Figure 6, we are reminded of the outline of adult representation.

The mentor concept has been implemented for the purpose of modeling effective adult behavior. Often, the role of mentor is limited to giving the child exposure to a specific body of knowledge, skill, process, and values appropriate to a chosen career or occupation. The other three characteristics represented in Figure 6 often remain covertly represented or wholly neglected. Good *psychosocial modeling* must also be available. Parents can often play this part, but teachers and other significant intimates might consciously work to represent originality, persistence, and personal integration as well as occupational competence.

With this backdrop of goals for psychosocial development, counsel and guidance provided during the transition to successful adulthood can be elaborated. Counsel and guidance can be provided by many in a youngster's life. Certainly, parents and friends serve this purpose. But during particular times, we look to professional sources of assistance.

THE ROLE OF COUNSELORS AND PSYCHOSOCIAL PERSONNEL

Historically, psychosocial service personnel interested in the gifted have proposed the domain of emotional and social development to be their special responsibility, their curriculum. They recognize that the eventual realization of a person's exceptional potential in the form of mature accomplishment is as much a function of that person's psychological well-being as it is a consequence of his or her intellect, creativity, or motivation. Therefore, the active participation of counselors and other psychosocial personnel is an essential feature of an effective differentiated educational program for gifted, creative, and talented children and youth.

Within schools, these professionals have generally accepted, as a major part of their role, the facilitation of healthy personality and behavior, allowing the individual to integrate successfully into the larger adult roles of family life and work (Blocher, 1974). Functional mental health is best sponsored by psychosocial programming focused on the development of high levels of self-awareness in individuals. This awareness includes knowledge of unique abilities and skills applicable to lives in which the actualization of self unfolds in innovative forms contributive to the individual and to society as a whole. As Sanborn (1978) wrote:

> A counseling and guidance approach calls for highly individualized contracts and interpretations.... One of the main purposes of counseling and guidance in the schools is to discover unique patterns of individual characteristics—interests, aptitudes, abilities, values, motives—and to assist the individual to determine the meaning of these characteristics in relation to educational, career, and life style opportunities.

Articulation of the role of this type of counseling and guidance with gifted youngsters dates back to the late 1950s, as described in Rothney and Kooperman's article, "Guidance for the Gifted" (1958). Using a trait factor model of psychological practice, they defined the principle role of the psychosocial professional as assisting the child in carefully evaluating his or her particular resources and matching that individual pattern of talents and interests to appropriate educational and vocational choices. This traditional role for counseling personnel can be traced directly to the beginning of the profession with Parson's (1909) Vocational Center in Boston at the beginning of this century.

The central theme of the Rothney/Kooperman statement is summed up in their following comment: "Counseling the gifted does not differ in nature from the counseling of other students, but it does vary in its demands on the counselor." These special demands include an appreciation of the effects on the child of accelerated cognitive and affective development, multipotential career decision patterns, and the need for special access to the adult world. The psychological factors of ability, creativity, motivation, and self-concept in the gifted should be integrated during accomplishment of these psychosocial tasks, and the counseling process must be atuned to the process of developmental integration.

Differential Programming

Following on the heels of Rothney/Kooperman, Gowan (1960) presented a slightly elaborated version of the same theme. In perhaps the most quoted of all articles on guidance of the gifted, "Organization of Guidance for Gifted Children," he sounded a general call for psychosocial professionals to become familiar with the special needs of the gifted, sponsoring the notion of a less directive, more client-centered view of clinical work with this group. In time, Gowan's thinking came to be the central focus in formulating a counsel and guidance framework for the gifted and talented. Perhaps his most articulate argument is his consistent plea for "differentiated" programs of counsel and guidance for the gifted, built upon the assumption of developmental discontinuities between themselves and their age peers.

More recent advocates for differentiated psychosocial services, including Colangelo and Zaffrann (1979), Perrone and Male (1981), and Bruch (1975), have advanced the particulars of planful interventions. Each has taken his or her own special tack in relation to the special needs of gifted and talented individuals. But none departs radically from the two principle traditions of *scholarship* and *practice*—Rothney's trait factor/ career approach and Gowan's client-centered, affective focus—first suggested for the field.

Specific Goals and Interventions

In the tradition of expansion and elaboration, Figure 7 presents a set of specific goals and concomitant psychosocial practices that can be useful for psychosocial service personnel who work with the gifted. Each proposed intervention flows from the humanistic propositions regarding personality development and behavior, as elaborated by Maslow and other third-force psychologists, and is a specific extension of the general model of transition toward individual excellence depicted in Figure 6. Each intervention is correlated with a particular goal appropriate to the individual's overall psychosocial development.

None of these goals, or any of the related interventions, is peculiarly appropriate to psychosocial education of the gifted. Each and all are as meaningful to working with any individual as to working with this special population. Yet, the application with the gifted appears to have special utility.

Self-Concept Separate from Products/Non-Product Relationship
"What did you do in school today?" or its variant, "How did you do in school today?" are perhaps the most frequently asked

---

FIGURE 7
Specific Goals and Selected Psychosocial Interventions

Specific Goals in the Psychosocial Development of the Gifted Individual	Selected Psychosocial Interventions to Facilitate Attainment of the Goals
* a self-concept separate from products	non-product relationship
* an orientation to hard work and task persistence	task-capacity match and a continuity of task involvement
* a capacity for constructive failure	honest brokering of critical feedback
* an affective-aesthetic sensitivity	"now" experiences
* effective social skills	interpersonal skills training
* a developmental peerage	planned developmental peer groups
* selection of an appropriate career or occupation	specialized career planning

questions greeting gifted children when they return home. Music lessons, report cards, test scores, and the answers to brain teasers are just some of the many products that serve as a primary criterion in dealing with the gifted. As a result of these repeated foci on outcomes, the individual can easily adopt a personal belief that "I am what I make." Such a personal rubric is psychologically neurotic because one's self-concept becomes tied directly to external evaluation by other people. The locus of psychological control has been allowed to migrate outside, making the individual susceptible to what Rogers (1954) has referred to as "conditions of worth." These conditions deny the inherent and unimpeachable worthiness of the individual and make this fundamental aspect of psychological well-being conditional on the evaluation of others, especially one's intimates.

As a counter to this proclivity of intimates, a major feature of any psychosocial intervention with the gifted must be to establish a non-product relationship. This term is a specialized label for the person-centered relationship advocated in the therapeutic writing of Rogers (1959). The non-product relationship is best established by utilizing interpersonal skills, as outlined in writings of practitioners such as Ginott (1965) and Gordon (1970). The basics of this type of relationship have been defined in detail by Rogers, who cogently argued that its establishment and maintenance between intimates facilitates "man's tendency to actualize himself, to become his potentialities." Individuals are not legitimized by their products but, rather, by the inherent tendency toward *becoming* through an openness to experience and an affirmation of their inherent right to serve as the locus of evaluation.

These characteristics of individual experience are nurtured by relationships typified by *psychological safety* and *freedom*. A sense of safety is sponsored when the individual's intimates regard him or her as having unconditional worth, when the relationship is devoid of judgments and evaluations by the other person or persons, and when the intimates empathically understand the individual's experience. When the relationship is also characterized by a complete freedom of the participants to speak of all feelings and ideas no matter what their content, focus, or intensity, yet all are required to act in a responsible fashion, the experiential components of a non-profit relationship are in place.

Orientation to Hard Work and Task Persistence/Task-Capacity
Match and Continuity of Task Involvement

Thomas Edison's statement that genius is 99% perspiration
and 1% inspiration captures the essence of the hard work required to achieve individual excellence. But hard work in itself
is not sufficient for such attainment. Persistence at a task is
also a requisite. Much hard work goes for naught if it is dispersed
across too many tasks. Excellence is achieved through consci-
entious effort in a single direction over long periods of time.
This perspective, however, is the antithesis of what individuals
experience in our society. Distraction and variety are typical of
our day-to-day experience. Seldom do young people encounter
the need to work hard at a single task over an extended time.
Distractibility (Klein, 1983) and low motivation (Whitmore,
1981), not surprisingly, are often characteristic of individuals
who are gifted.

Many strategems can be offered to address these dual goals
of establishing an orientation to hard work and fostering persistence in gifted youngsters. Two requisites of psychosocial quality are to make certain that the performance demands of the
task at hand match the child's capacity to perform, and that a
continuity of involvement is sustained with that same task. The
effect of both these interventions can be enhanced by allowing
the child to self-select the task (Renzulli, 1977).

When the task and capacity are mismatched, motivation to
work is lowered. The mismatch can be in either direction. If the
task to be accomplished far supersedes the child's capacity to
perform, personal motivation will be low; if the reverse is the
case, the effect will be the same. This latter profile more often
than not represents the experience of gifted children in schools.

In contrast, the best circumstance is when the task to be
done barely supersedes the capacity to perform. Then a
person's motivation to work at the task will be at its highest.
The child's hard work is reinforced by the opportunity to stay
with the task over an extended time. One way to manage this in
schools is to design curriculum activities in a manner so that
the youngsters would do the task, hand it in, receive an evaluation, and then redo the task toward a higher level of excellence,
as outlined through the evaluation. This performance–evalua-

tion–performance feedback loop is repeated, always spiraling upward in quality. Not all school activities lend themselves to this process, but certainly some do. These should be used as the medium to carry the affective, attitudinal message of the import of hard work and task persistence to the eventual realization of individual excellence.

Capacity for Constructive Failure/
Honest Brokering of Critical Feedback

In Saul Bass's film *Why Man Creates,* which he produced for Kaiser Aluminum, are a series of interviews with a collection of scientists in which they are encouraged to discuss their experience as innovators. Much of their commentary tells about the long years they have spent working with singular commitment toward solution of problems including world hunger and the like. Their words are impressive testimony to the necessity for hard work and persistence.

The last interview is with a scientist who has worked for years on the problem of cancer. Near the end of his remarks, he reveals that he has just become aware that all the effort has gone for naught; he and his colleagues have found out that their proposed solution has run up against a blank wall. This failure is all the more compelling because it stands in stark contrast to the film's previous examples of success.

Yet, the message of the vignette is not over with the revelation of the failure. The final exchange between the narrator and the scientist is most revealing: "Well, what are you going to do now?" "I don't know." Rather than being a statement of discouragement, we are sure he will continue his search, for as he says, "We have hit a blank wall *for now.*" "For now" puts the failure into perspective as a temporary thing. This perseverence in the face of failure is the essence of hope and a constructive attitude toward the trials of life. The scientist's statement represents a powerful capacity of the mature individual to move beyond failure toward success, even to use the failure as a stepping stone to that success. Excellence is not attained on the first try. The high bar falls off more often than it stays up when a jumper is pressing the limit of his or her capacity. This ability to use failure constructively, to transcend, must be deeply embedded in the attitudes and affect of the individual.

Yet gifted youngsters frequently are not educated to do this important thing. Because much of what they are asked to do often does not tax performance capacity, easy success is the usual outcome of action. At most, this poor task/capacity match sponsors low intrinsic motivation and, at best, high instrumental motivation. When the latter develops, youngsters stop doing things for any inherent value in the activity itself, and work for what other things it gets for them. In school, these other things are usually grades, class rank, and the like. For those who invest themselves in this instrumental pattern of extrinsic reward, their payoff is often a consistent string of superior evaluations in the form of As or 100s or the equivalent. Perfection becomes the goal and perfectionism the attitude. This is detrimental to development of a capacity for successful failure, which is so central to the attainment of individual excellence.

Certainly, careful attention to task/capacity match is conducive to achieving this psychosocial goal. Yet, by itself, it is not sufficient because to turn failure into a stepping stone requires an ability to evaluate one's actions honestly and in detail. Attaining such sophisticated skills is best learned through involvement with intimates who choose to act as honest brokers of one's behavior, telling the individual their view of his or her performance in elaborated detail, using good critical feedback. The critical feedback is characterized by a set of rules for its use, such as making sure that it is specific and immediate instead of general and deferred, that it is descriptive and behavioral rather than judgmental and inferential. This critical feedback provides the child an expanded view of his or her action and a framework for rectifying the failure—a failure that now is not final but has taken on the texture of the latest trial in a series of efforts toward the goal of excellence.

Affective-Aesthetic Sensitivity/"Now" Experiences
The pursuit of excellence in life requires more than a collective view of beauty. It requires a personal sensitivity and standard of quality emerging not from committee caucuses but from that internal frame of reference and evaluation indigenous to a

secure yet flexible self-concept. A primary feature of such a psychic state is the capacity for *peak experience*—the name Maslow gave to that state of integrated awareness, highly affective in quality, in which the individual engages the immediacy of the moment. Internal dimensions of time and space are experienced as being as legitimate and understandable as the time and space typical of the external world of objects and events. Here, aesthetic qualities of universality, focus, and singularity constitute the meaningful dimensions of knowing and lead to those creative intuitions so central to mature originality and innovation.

Affective and subjective qualities of the phenomenon are located in the temporal immediacy of the moment. The capacity of the individual to be present with the moment as it is occurring right now, however, is discouraged by the circumstances of day-to-day living and the expanded role of past and future in modern, post-industrial life. These detrimental factors are enhanced in gifted youngsters by our advocacy of activities such as futurism and by our enthusiasm for their developing sophisticated cognitive, analytical skills. Thus, deflected from an integrated awareness of self in the moment, the gifted are most prone to divorce themselves from their intuitions, losing access to the capacity to sense the bud of the gestalt, the growing tip of the new idea or action.

Various "now" experiences can be designed into the activities of gifted youngsters to preserve and elaborate this innate human capacity. Guided imagery is one of a series of possible techniques. Meditation, selected yoga activities, and biofeedback are additional aids to accomplish this end. These, however, are only mechanisms to access the process and to educate about the process. They are not the process that occurs within the framework of daily events, and these activities must not become a kind of replacement for the real thing.

Effective Social Skills/Interpersonal Skills Training

Hollingworth (1942) said that the subjects of her study, individuals with IQs of 180 or higher, must learn to "suffer fools gladly." Blunt as this may sound, it captures an aspect of living for them. The comment applies to others as well. Often the developmental discontinuity established between gifted children and their chronological peers because of developmental acceleration creates a social vacuum in which the social skills of effective living are not easily learned. The capacity for empathic understanding may be rich in the individual but of little use because he or she has not learned good listening skills or how to confront others without argumentation and anger.

The import of developing this repertoire of skills has been amplified in today's world because the complexity of many of the problems requires a collective response rather than one person's lonely efforts. Cherry (1966) noted that the last man to know everything was the mathematician and philosopher Leibnitz. In one way or another, innovation and productivity are dependent acts in today's world. Interpersonal skills training, therefore, should include work on small group dynamics. Many resources exist for developing psychosocial curriculum for this purpose. Pfeiffer and Jones' (1982) *Handbook for Group Facilitators* and Johnson and Johnson's (1975) *Joining Together* are two examples of this literature.

Developmental Peerage/Planned Developmental Peer Group

As has been noted repeatedly, gifted childen have a developmental discontinuity in relation to their peers. The disparity between how gifted younsters experience the world and how their age mates experience it often becomes so great that the individual feels at first different and then alone and isolated. This isolation may become the birthplace of dysfunctional self-perceptions and social behaviors.

A constructive response to the possibility is to assist gifted individuals in establishing a developmental peerage—an association with others of like mind and experience. As the saying goes, "Birds of a feather flock together." Our society, however, tends to structure the social and intellectual experiences of young people around time rather than developmental readiness. Although efficient, this lockstep practice is not effective, especially in nurturing the psychosocial growth of gifted youngsters.

Planned developmental peer groups stand as a viable alternative to this restrictive practice. Homogeneous grouping based on intellectual or performance readiness is the most frequent example of developmental peer groups, though the strategy is not usually employed for psychosocial reasons. Yet, one of the favorable spin-offs of this practice is that the youngsters begin to recognize that they are not alone in either their intellectual performance or their psychosocial concerns. The experience of developmental discontinuity is reduced, though not eradicated, and the youngster experiences a sense of *universality*. This is a therapeutic feature of group experiences defined by Yalom (1975) as one of the "curative factors" inherent in well planned psychosocial counseling groups.

Yalom's approach to developmental peer group work elaborates this set of psychosocial factors unique to such group work. He has argued that this uniqueness arises primarily from the social dynamics of the group itself and cannot be generated in one-to-one relationships, no matter how positive and intimate. Others do not hold such a specialized view of group work, but all argue for the developmentally constructive nature of planned group work (Corey & Corey, 1983). Certainly, these group counseling models offer a unique opportunity to intervene in the lives of gifted youngsters and address the potentially maladaptive aspects of developmental discontinuity in an organized and facilitative manner.

Selection of Appropriate Career or Occupation/ Specialized Career Planning

We have all been confronted by the difficult question of what we are going to be when we grow up. Many of us have come to be what we are occupationally by convoluted routes, guided more often by circumstance than by plan and intent. Career/ occupational choice of gifted individuals, their selection of the specific domain of performance in which they intend to pursue excellence, is as complex for them as it is for others. Its complexity, however, is often enhanced by certain aspects of their giftedness. They encounter the same psychosocial developmental question as we all do, but their encounter is unique. Numerous statements have been made outlining this vocational experience (Milne, 1979) and organizing planful response (Van-Tassel-Baska, 1981). Among the many factors involved in the

process are one's multipotentiality, early career choice, selection
of careers that do not exist, and the need to find occupations
allowing for innovation.

Multipotentiality points to the complexity of deciding what
to be when one can be many things. When the career decision
process revolves around answering the question, "What are you
going to be when you grow up?" it becomes a perplexity for individuals who can do many things yet believe they must do only
one. The new career development models that acknowledge the
legitimacy of multiple careers using a life-span developmental
approach are quite useful in dealing with this aspect of the individual's psychosocial experience.

In contrast to the deferred decision process typical of multipotentiality, some youngsters make career choices early in life
and pursue the choice in a single-minded fashion, frustrating
our American ideal of the well-rounded person, doing lots of
things and hopefully doing them all quite well—a sort of "jack
of all trades" notion. Perhaps the best current example of this
pattern of early intense focus is seen in the computer whizzes,
who are often highlighted in the popular press. Bloom and Sosniak's (1981) work on eminent persons supports the importance
of early choice in individual lives. A readiness on the part of
others to deal constructively with a pattern of concentrated effort is vital to its realization, however much it runs in the face of
our preference for more broad-based and extended career decision making.

At times gifted youngsters pursue careers that do not
exist. Their occupations are in the future. A good example of
this is a young girl who plans to be an electrical engineer on an
internationally manned space station. That occupation does not
exist yet. This is a predicament as most career education
models depend heavily on modeling careers for children so they
can begin to compare their preferences and interests with those
characteristic of a particular occupation. Most career assessment procedures are based on such an antecedent, comparative
model. So this girl's pursuit of her career selection has to be to a
large degree an original act. She became fluent in Esperanto on
the assumption that she would need a universal language to
communicate with the linguistically diverse community of the

station. She spent a summer with NASA hanging up space suits so she could be around others who had like interests. Her vocational efforts are a series of original choices guided by good judgment, based on a lot of speculative thinking.

Another vital aspect of the vocational choices of individuals who are intent upon transforming their lives toward excellence is the investigation of occupational niches that allow for innovation and productivity. Addressing this directly during career counseling and career education seems a valuable component of an overall model of specialized services for these young people.

Goals/Practices In Relation to the Model

When viewed in relation to the larger model for the transformation toward excellence outlined in Figure 6, each of these specific goals and their respective psychosocial practices expand the model in the direction of skills and practices necessary for relating effectively to the unique developmental experience of gifted children. Our aim is to help them toward their individual expression of excellence in adult life. Accomplishing this end requires long, complex, and planful involvement by those the child considers as his or her intimates. The goal is the realization of a mature pattern of personality and behavior that aids the individual in acting on his or her talent in a personally meaningful, yet socially responsible fashion.

Often, the usual effort needed to realize this end is justified by holding forth on the importance of discovering and developing people who will provide us with the great ideas and accomplishments to come, the future Curies, Einsteins, van Goghs, and Jeffersons. But the worth of our efforts for the gifted need not pivot on the eventual realization of genius. The realization of "ordinary excellence" is sufficient justification for our efforts. As a society, our well-being is just as dependent upon the day-to-day expressions of commonplace excellence, such as that of a fine classroom teacher or an active, thoughtful town council member, as it is upon the realization of brilliant insight and innovation. The expression of individual excellence in ordinary, mundane walks of life is of great importance, because through such expressions the well-being of the social infrastructure of our lives is assured. Through the ordinary and mundane, most of us find the means to fulfill our individual potential. Here is found the basis for living an innovative life that exceeds the limits of previous lives. As Goethe has said:

> The hour has sixty minutes in store,
> the day a thousand and more,
> Now figure out my little son,
> All the things that can be done.

SUMMARY

This chapter presents the framework for helping a child toward his or her own individual expression of excellence. Its focus is on transformation of exceptional potential into a defined, productive talent and on the things adults can do to facilitate the transformation.

Special consideration is given to psychosocial aspects of this process, with particular attention directed at issues such as motivation, interpersonal skills, and career planning. Each of these issues is discussed in relation to certain unique features of personal development characteristic of gifted, creative, and talented youngsters.

REFERENCES

Albert, R. Exceptionally gifted boys and their parents. *Gifted Child Quarterly,* 1980, *24*(1), 174-179.

Blocher, D. *Developmental counseling.* New York: Ronald Press, 1974.

Bloom, B., & Sosniak, L. Talent development versus schooling. *Educational Leadership,* 1981, *39,* 85-94.

Bruch, C. Assessment of creativity in culturally different children. *Gifted Child Quarterly,* 1975, *19*(2).

Cherry, C. *On human communication.* Cambridge, MA: M.I.T. Press, 1966.

Colangelo, N., & Zaffrann, R. *New voices in counseling the gifted.* Dubuque, IA: Kendall/Hunt, 1979.

Corey, G., & Corey, M. *Theory and practice of group counseling* (3rd ed.). Monterey, CA: Brooks/Cole, 1983.

Dambrowski, K. *Positive disintegration.* Boston: Little, Brown, 1964.

Delisle, J. Striking out: Suicide and the gifted adolescent. *G/C/T,* 1982, *24*(10), 16-19.

Dweck, C. The role of expectations and attributions in the alleviation of learned helplessness. *Journal of Personality & Social Psychology,* 1975, *31*(4), 674-685.

Erickson, E. *Childhood and society.* New York: Norton, 1950.

Feldman, D. (Ed.). *Developmental approaches to giftedness and creativity.* San Francisco: Jossey-Bass, 1982.

Foster, W. Self concept, intimacy, and the attainment of excellence. *Journal for the Education of the Gifted,* 1982, *5*(3).

Foster, W., & Gatto, P. Parenting the gifted child. *Illinois Council for the Gifted Newsletter,* 1980, *5*(2).

Fox, L. Sex differences in mathematical precocity: Bridging the gap. In D.P. Keating (Ed.), *Intellectual talent: Research and development.* Baltimore: Johns Hopkins University Press, 1976.

Fromm, E. *Man for himself.* New York: Holt, Rinehart & Winston, 1947.

Ginott, H. *Between parent and child.* New York: Avon Books, 1965.

Gordon, T. *Parent effectiveness training.* New York: Wyden, 1970.

Gowan, J. Organization of guidance for gifted children. *Personnel & Guidance Journal,* 1960, *39*(4), 275-279.

Gowan, J. Background and history of the gifted-child movement. In J. Stanley, W. George, & C. Solono (Eds.), *The gifted and creative: A fifty-year perspective.* Baltimore: Johns Hopkins University Press, 1977.

Hall, E. *The silent language.* Garden City, NY: Anchor Books, 1973.

Havighurst, R. *Human development and education.* New York: Longmans, 1953.

Hollingworth, L. *Children above 180 IQ.* New York: World Book, 1942.

Johnson, D., & Johnson, F. *Joining together.* Englewood Cliffs, NJ: Prentice-Hall, 1975.

Klein, J. Underachievers: The two-type hypotheses. Unpublished doctoral dissertation, Rutgers University, 1983.

Maslow, A. *Toward a psychology of being* (2nd ed.). New York: Van Nostrand Reinhold, 1968.

Milne, B. Career education. In H. Passow (Ed.), *The gifted and talented: Their education and development* (78th yearbook of the National Society for the Study of Education, Part 1). Chicago: University of Chicago Press, 1979.

Montour, K. William James Sidis, the broken twig. *American Psychologist,* April 1977, pp. 265-279.

Parsons, F. *Choosing a vocation.* Boston: Houghton Mifflin, 1909.

Perrone, R., & Male, R. *The developmental education and guidance of talented learners.* Rockville, MD: Aspen Systems Press, 1981.

Pfeiffer, J., & Jones, J. *1982 annual handbook for group facilitators.* LaJolla, CA: University Associates, 1982.

Piaget, J. *The psychology of intelligence.* Totowa, NJ: Littlefield, Adams, 1960.

Piechowski, M. Self-actualization as a developmental structure: A profile of Antoine de Saînt-Exupéry. *Genetic Psychology Monographs,* 1983, *97.*

Pressey, S. Concerning the nature and nurture of genius. *Scientific Monthly,* 1955, *81,* 123-129.

Renzulli, J. *The enrichment triad.* Wethersfield, CT: Creative Learning Press, 1977.

Renzulli, J. What makes giftedness? Reexamining a definition. *Phi Delta Kappan,* 1978, *60*(3), 180-184.

Richert, S. *Affective education.* Sewell, NJ: EIC–South, 1983.

Rogers, C. Toward a theory of creativity. ETC, 1954, *11,* 250-258.

Rogers, C. A theory of therapy, personality, and interpersonal relationships, as developed in the client-centered framework. In S. Koch (Ed.), *Psychology: A study of a science.* New York: McGraw-Hill, 1959.

Rothney, J., & Kooperman, N. Guidance of the gifted. In R. Havighurst (Ed.), *Education for the gifted* (57th yearbok of the National Society for the Study of Education, Part 2). Chicago: University of Chicago Press, 1958.

Sanborn, M. Differential counseling needs of the gifted and talented. In N. Colangelo & R. Zaffrann (Eds.), *New voices in counseling the gifted.* Dubuque, IA: Kendall/Hunt, 1978.

Seidlin, O. Liberty and self-control: Goethe's vision of a new world. *Imprimis,* 1982, *11*(5), 1-6.

Silverman, L. Personality development: The pursuit of excellence. *Journal for the Education of the Gifted,* 1982, *5*(3).

VanTassel-Baska, J. A comprehensive model of career education for gifted. *Journal of Career Education,* 1981, *7*(4), pp. 325-331.

Whitmore, J. The etiology of underachievement in highly gifted young children. *Journal for the Education of the Gifted,* 1981, *3*(1), 38-51.

Yalom, I. *The theory and practice of group psychotherapy* (2nd ed.). New York: Basic Books, 1975.

Evaluating Programs for Gifted Learners

Ken Seeley

The discussion of program evaluation in this chapter is both descriptive and prescriptive. It centers on the critical issues in evaluation, from this writer's perspective.

WHAT IS THE PURPOSE OF PROGRAM EVALUATION?

"The general purpose of evaluation is to gather, analyze and disseminate information that can be used to make decisions about educational programs" (Renzulli, 1975, p. 2). In any discussion of evaluation, we must examine the area of decision making. Further, we rarely encounter situations in which only one simple decision is to be made (e.g., to continue a program for the gifted or to drop it). Rather, evaluation provides information for a series of interactive decisions that are typically directed toward program improvement. The decisions themselves should also be subject to evaluation such that evaluation and decision making continue to intertwine in the evolution of a program. The evaluation is the "bottom line" for creating defensible programs.

WHAT IS THE DECISION MAKING PROCESS?

Decision making is "...a process influenced by information and values, whereby a perceived problem is explicitly defined, alternative solutions are posed and weighted, and a choice is made that subsequently is implemented and evaluated" (Lipham & Furth, 1976, p. 2). Gorton (1980) has presented the following model for the process of decision making:

Step 1—Define the situation.

Step 2—Identify the alternatives.

Step 3—Assess the alternatives.

Step 4—Select the best possible alternative.

Step 5—Secure acceptance of the situation.

Step 6—Implement the decision.

Step 7—Evaluate the decision.

This model assists us in examining where and how evaluation interfaces with decision making. In the initial phase of need for a decision, the evaluation should attend to *why* evaluate a particular component of a program and should tell us *who* the audience should be for the information [the decision maker(s)]. Step 1, in defining the situation, should guide the evaluation so as to accurately describe the status quo, not only "where we are" but in what context the program being evaluated is presently functioning.

Steps 2 and 3 are often not a part of program evaluation, but should be. Renzulli (1975, p. 6) suggested that one important step in any evaluation is to "...suggest realistic, as well as ideal, alternative courses of action." Gorton has pointed out that decision makers often consider only two alternatives and see these alternatives in an "either-or" context. The evaluation should recommend a number of alternatives and the possible permutations that might be considered. A serious fallacy in assessing alternatives "...lies in making decisions without prior examination of the assumptions which lie at the heart of the feasibility of each alternative" (Gorton, 1980, p. 232). (Later in this chapter a model addressing this concern will be presented.) Too often, evaluations do not touch on the underlying assumptions of key features of the program being evaluated. The evaluation then tends to address surface symptoms, and resulting recommendations do not effect positive change.

Step 4 in the decision making process, selecting the best alternative, should be apparent if the previous steps have been followed. If one course of action is not clearly the best, Step 3 should be repeated. Rarely is an "ideal" alternative at hand but, rather, the "best" of what seems possible with the given constraints.

Steps 5 and 6 require the highest level of diplomacy in decision making. Securing acceptance of a decision, and then implementing it, is much easier if the evaluation is done well to provide the supporting data. No decision regarding program change will be universally accepted by those affected. Nevertheless, the decision maker with good evaluation data can provide a defensible position and should be able to describe the steps and alternatives that went into the final decision.

The final steps in decision making cycle back through a comprehensive evaluation system to examine the impact of a program decision. For example, if a decision were made to change the identification process for gifted by raising standards to produce fewer students, the impact of that decision should be a part of the evaluation for next year's program. The evaluation plan must be sensitive to the critical decisions that impact the program. Informal feedback is usually appropriate for minor decisions.

The interplay of evaluation and decision making is essential to design of the evaluation plan. Those responsible for evaluation must attend to this relationship if we are to obtain the best information in the formation of defensible programs for gifted learners.

WHAT IS THE DIFFERENCE BETWEEN RESEARCH AND EVALUATION?

A philosophical perspective of this writer is in order, to differentiate evaluation from research. The philosophy is that evaluation design must be an integral part of program development such that each facet of evaluation relates to program objectives or anticipated outcomes. Therefore, evaluation provides decision making information regarding how close a program comes to its predetermined standards. The resulting discrepancies allow decision makers to address program improvement needs.

The philosophical perspective on research is that a comparison is implicit. For example, a research design would be needed to determine if independent study were more effective than resource room intervention in accelerating the social studies curriculum. Research requires approaches different from evaluation approaches. Research designs are needed to make comparisons in order to control variables. Statistical analysis is also required to account for variance or relationships that may exist in comparing groups or approaches. This dichotomy is drawn here to caution program evaluators who attempt to answer research questions without adequate designs to answer those questions. Certainly research is needed and can be included as part of an evaluation design. But different standards must be used in designing research than those used for evaluation.

Evaluation as described here is usually sufficient to address demands of decision makers in school settings. If decision makers want a comparative study, research is required with all its attendant standards and procedures. Research is usually more time consuming and costly to carry out than is evaluation.

The critical issue in differentiating research from evaluation appears when evaluators attempt to answer research questions with evaluation designs not intended to provide research data. Decisions are then based on designs that did not adequately control variables or adequately analyze comparative data. The classic example of a research question that uses evaluation designs, with unsuccessful answers, is, "Is enrichment better than acceleration for gifted students?" A comparative study must be done to answer this question.

WHAT INSTRUMENTATION IS NEEDED FOR EVALUATION?

Instruments are needed to gather data for evaluation. Instruments have a broad definition for purposes of this discussion. They can range from a structured interview with parents to a *WISC-R.* The purpose of instruments is to measure and describe a condition or level of performance. Instruments also imply recording data in some systematic manner.

Critical issues for evaluation reside in two areas of instrumentation and measurement. The first issue is the *appropriateness* of the instrument to provide pertinent and meaningful information for the evaluation. The second issue is the *interpretation and presentation of data* gathered by instruments.

The field of gifted education is replete with teacher-made evaluation instruments. These typically survey students, parents, teachers, mentors, and administrators to gain their perceptions of the gifted program. These data are aggregated into a report upon which decisions are made concerning program modification and maintenance. Often these "soft" data are supplemented with "hard" data from standardized tests of achievement, intelligence, and/or creativity.

Although this framework for evaluation is sound conceptually, it is too often done with instruments that are subject to a good deal of measurement error. The soft data from teacher-made surveys can provide excellent descriptive information for program administrators, but these data are global and are too often interpreted as specific. Groups of respondents are compared to each other using different instruments, resulting in measurement error. For instance, a student may respond to the survey item, "How did you like the unit on computer-based retrieval systems (Rate 1–5)." The parents might be asked to respond to, "Rate your child's attitudes toward computer usage (Rate 1–5)." Although these items are similar in some ways and provide some descriptive data, they are different enough that comparisons should not be made. Yet we find mean scores extrapolated from samples of the population, upon which decisions are made concerning the use of computers in the gifted program. Unfortunately, measurement errors persist and impact on evaluation.

Even hard data from standardized measures are subject to abuse in both use and interpretation. In gifted education we continue to wrestle with balancing hard data against soft data. Hard data are seen as test scores and quantifiable measures. Soft data usually consist of observations, rating scales, and professional judgments. The ceiling effects of achievement tests and the variations and biases of intelligence tests and creativity tests confound decision making.

An example of a frequently used intelligence test is the *Slosson.* Although it shares many items with the *Stanford-Binet* and is correlated with the *Binet,* it does not provide equivalent scores. The meaning of the scores cannot be established because the norming sample was not from a normal population but was a collection of referred cases. The reliability of the test is unknown. The coefficient reported in the manual was obtained for a "clinical sample" of 200 persons whose IQ scores averaged 84. These data are not very hard. Those who determine measures should be aware of all the technical data from the instruments used, as well as the underlying conceptual theories on which the test is based.

This discussion is not intended to dissuade anyone from using both soft and hard data in evaluating programs. Rather, we must attend to the measurement problems inherent in using any kind of instruments and guard against sweeping generalizations upon which important decisions are to be made. We must use all the data we can gather to create defensible programs for gifted children. But the measurement and interpretation must be done well with good instruments that attend both to the focus of the evaluation and to the audience for the evaluation. Principles of *validity* and *reliability* should be addressed in all instruments. Local norms that attend to these principles can be established for frequently used instruments.

WHAT CONSTITUTES EXCELLENCE IN EVALUATION?

The model guidelines in Figure 8 represent a synthesis of ideas and concepts from these major authors in educational evaluation: Gage (1970), Stake and Denny (1969), and Stufflebeam (1971).The major areas to be addressed in planning comprehensive educational evaluation are: (1) context of the evaluation, (2) audience for the evaluation, (3) classes of decisions to be made, (4) usefulness of evaluation information, and (5) ethical considerations. These areas should guide the formulation of evaluation objectives, design, instrumentation, data gathering, and dissemination of results.

Context of the evaluation refers to the setting, including both people and program. Front-end analysis by the evaluator is necessary to determine attitudes of the audience toward the evaluation process. These attitudes can determine the accuracy of data sources and the level of openness to evaluation information. The context also attends to variations within and between programs. Rarely is a program not impacted by other programs. The interactive effects of programs should be part of the context description. Finally, the roles and goals of the evaluator and audience have to be made explicit during the course of the evaluation. The audience may expect a summative evaluation when a formative evaluation would be more appropriate.

Audience for the evaluation greatly affects formulation of the evaluation design. If the audience is homogeneous, with similar needs for information, gathering and reporting data are easier and more focused. If there are a number of different audiences, the design should differentiate objectives, methods, and reporting procedures.

Classes of decisions to be made from the evaluation are important determiners of methodology. Some decision makers may need to know only if intervention in a program is needed or not needed. Other decision makers may want the evaluation to produce a pool of data that can be drawn on for a specific reaction to a decision request. Such a data pool is important for planning decisions that require a number of alternatives. Adoption decisions that are based on data from other successful programs elsewhere and could be transported for adoption locally are often necessary. The final class of decisions is individual versus group decisions. Data for individual decision makers can be directed to the decision maker's needs, but when decisions are to be made by groups, the evaluator must attend to various levels and types of information required by group members.

The usefulness of evaluation information is perhaps the hallmark of good evaluation practice. Too often evaluation is seen as an "add-on" activity to meet minimal accountability demands. In these situations decisions are based on limited information from selective sources that do not represent relevant constituencies.

To be useful, evaluation data must be valid and reliable. The scientific nature of the data gathering and analysis lends credibility to the results. This information should be relevant to the audiences in its application to program decisions. The most precise evaluation data are useless if they do not translate into effective decisions significant to program management. The evaluator must assist the audience in weighing the significance of data when applied to specific conditions. Audiences tend to infer significance to specific situations from data that are not directly applicable. These types of inference error result in poor decisions. The scope of the evaluation must be sufficiently broad to address the evaluation problems. Credibility of the data must be considered from both cognitive and affective dimensions. Evaluation information can be well-founded, but sensitivity to its impact on people should guide its format for reporting. Timeliness is another important component of how useful evaluation data are viewed. The information should be available when needed for decision making but also reported when the audience is most open to receive it.

The final dimension of usefulness of the evaluation is efficiency. Often evaluation demands exceed resources. The evaluator must assist the audience in setting priorities with attendant costs, so that the most useful information can be gathered for the best financial value.

Ethical considerations must overlay all aspects of program evaluation. To this end, three areas should be considered: candor, confidentiality, and scientific caution. Candor requires openness and accuracy in gathering and reporting data. Confidentiality may have to be assured when providing certain information to different audiences. Scientific caution has to be a part of the interpretation, to limit inferences. Even the best instruments and statistical designs have limitations. Cautions must be clearly stated in reporting data.

Figure 8 synthesizes these major dimensions of evaluation into guidelines for reference. They constitute a comprehensive model for excellence in evaluation of educational programs.

FIGURE 8
Model Guidelines for Evaluation

Major Areas	Sub-Components	Comments
1. Context of the evaluation	1.1 *Attitudes* toward evaluation.	1.1 Evaluation raises anxiety and often negative attitudes.
	1.2 *Variations* within and between programs.	1.2 Programs being evaluated are rarely homogeneous within themselves.
	1.3 *Roles and goals* of evaluator and audience.	1.3 There must be a good match between evaluator and audience.

FIGURE 8
Continued

Major Areas	Sub-Components	Comments
2. Audience for the evaluation	2.1 *Single-channel reporting* to a person or group with the same information needs.	2.1 A homogeneous audience is helpful in identifying decisions, sources of information, and appropriate reporting procedures.
	2.2 *Multi-channel reporting* to several audiences.	2.2 Several audiences require separate considerations based on information needs for decisions.
3. Classes of decisions	3.1 *Intervention* information for decisions.	3.1 This is information for dichotomous decisions. Is intervention needed?
	3.2 *Reaction* information for decisions.	3.2 Information from evaluation data must allow for easy retrieval and reaction to a decision request.
	3.3 *Planning* information for decisions.	3.3 Planning decisions require a broad information base for viable alternatives.
	3.4 *Adoption* decision information requires knowledge of programs adopted elsewhere.	3.4 Adoption decisions are based on known, effective alternatives to be applied to local conditions.

FIGURE 8
Continued

Major Areas	Sub-Components	Comments
	3.5 *Individual vs. group decisions* require different evaluation data.	3.5 Individual decision information is attained with some certainty. Group decisions require attention to various levels and types of information for members of the group.
4. Usefulness of evaluation information	4.1 *Scientific nature* of data assists credibility.	4.1 The validity and reliability of the data should be made clear.
	4.2 *Relevance* of data makes it useful.	4.2 To be relevant, the data must apply to contingencies in meeting program objectives.
	4.3 *Significance* of data is its importance to making decisions.	4.3 Data must be weighted in its importance to specific conditions.
	4.4 *Scope* of data must cover evaluation problems.	4.4 Scope of the evaluation must key on its major elements related to necessary decisions.
	4.5 *Credibility* is the level perceived by the audience from the information.	4.5 The evaluator must consider the audience's cognitive and affective response to the evaluation data.

FIGURE 8
Continued

Major Areas	Sub-Components	Comments
	4.6 *Timeliness* is a major factor in usefulness of data.	4.6 Time has three dimensions in evaluation: lag time (time between information need and information available), time points (specific times when data are needed), and readiness (when the audience is most open to receive information).
	4.7 *Efficiency* of evaluation data refers to the financial value of information related to its usefulness.	4.7 The value of data to be gathered must be weighted based on cost of obtaining it. Priorities must be set by evaluator working with audience.
5. Ethical considerations	5.1 *Candor* is important to accuracy and completeness of information.	5.1 The evaluator should avoid unsupported judgments and biases and be candid with the audience.
	5.2 *Confidentiality* may have to be preserved from sharing information among different audiences.	5.2 The evaluator must be sensitive to when confidentiality can be and should be guaranteed in sharing evaluation data.

Major Areas	Sub-Components	Comments

FIGURE 8
Continued

Major Areas	Sub-Components	Comments
	5.3 *Scientific caution* should guide interpretation or inferences from data reported.	5.3 Limitations on inferences from the evaluation must be a part of the final evaluation report.

SUMMARY

This chapter has emphasized the relationship between evaluation and decision making. Programs for gifted students typically require higher levels of accountability than do ordinary education programs. These categorical programs are usually under closer scrutiny, with many evaluation questions implicit in the accountability demands. The dimension of decision making was explored here as it relates to evaluation and ultimately to accountability.

Much discussion is noted in the field of gifted education about creating "defensible" programs. At the heart of defensibility is good evaluation practice tied to good processes for decision making. The model guidelines (Figure 8) constitute good evaluation practice. As we move toward excellence in gifted education, we must attend to the best educational practices we have at hand.

REFERENCES

Gage, G. Distribution of information. In C.F. Paulson, *A strategy for evaluation design.* Salem: Oregon State System of Higher Education, April 1970.

Gorton, R.A. School administration and supervision. Dubuque, IA: William C. Brown Co., 1980, pp. 227-249.

Lipham, J.M., & Furth, M.L. *The principal and individually guided education.* Reading, MA: Addison-Wesley, 1976.

Renzulli, J. *A guidebook for evaluating programs for the gifted and talented.* Ventura, CA: Office of the County Superintendent of Schools, 1975.

Stake, R.E., & Denny, T. Needed concepts and techniques for utilizing more fully the potential of evaluation. In R.W. Tyler, *Educational evaluation: New roles, new means* (68th yearbook of the National Society for the Study of Education, Part 2). Chicago: University of Chicago Press, 1969.

Stufflebeam, D.L. *Educational evaluation and decision-making.* Itasca, IL: F.E. Peacock Publishers, 1971, pp. 49-105.

10
Summary

John Feldhusen

Proper education of gifted and talented youth calls for a large-scale effort by school personnel and parents. Much of the growth of school programs during the 1970s consisted of token efforts in which a single program service was held out by the schools as constituting a program for the gifted. An elementary pullout program offering 2 or 3 hours of instruction per week or a high school honors class in English have been offered as evidence of school programs. Parents, meanwhile, have sensed clearly from the reports their gifted children brought home from school that the needs of their children were not being met. Gifted children have complained of classes in which the subject matter was low-level and slow-paced. Gifted children have been required to spend many hours studying material they already knew, and even if the material to be learned was new, they would have to go through it at a pace appropriate for slow or average students.

Some schools have been unable to take any action to establish programs for the gifted and talented because of administrative resistance or incompetence. Many administrators, failing to recognize the obligation to provide a suitable education to meet the needs of all youth, have succumbed instead to fears of pressure from parents that programs for the gifted are elitist. That position apparently assumes that providing appropriate services for the gifted is somehow likely to foster the development of a social group that other students perceive as intellectually superior. Although athletic programs appear to be little concerned about this, it often arises in connection with the academic program. It is possible, of course, to use caution in labeling, categorizing, or glorifying the gifted and talented. The thousands of schools that have programs for the gifted seem to suffer no obvious problems of elitism.

MYTHS ABOUT THE GIFTED

The larger problem is perhaps incompetence or ignorance on the part of school personnel in many schools concerning characteristics, needs, program services and models, and curricula for the gifted and talented. In the absence of sound knowledge, a host of myths seems to dominate thinking concerning the gifted. These include: (1) they will succeed even if no service is provided, (2) if they are stimulated early in life, they will suffer burnout later, (3) identifying the gifted and talented is extremely difficult, and (4) they will experience social adjustment problems if they are placed in special programs. Schools that undertake substantial inservice programs and involve all personnel including administrators, counselors, and teachers overcome these problems and develop good program services for the gifted and talented.

PARENT INVOLVEMENT

Parental pressure has helped bring about programs for the gifted and talented in many schools. Formally organized parent groups have sprung up in thousands of communities. A large part of the membership of the National Association for Gifted Children and the membership of state organizations for the gifted consists of parents. These parents have "done their homework" in the sense that they have studied the literature in the gifted field and have become knowledgeable about gifted education—sometimes more so than school personnel.

PLANNING COMMITTEES

Perhaps the ideal approach to development of gifted programs has been the task force or planning committee, led by a strong, knowledgeable coordinator. These committees typically include teachers, administrators, counselors, parents, and sometimes gifted students. In addition to literature sources, these committees should have access to a consultant, and they should visit some good model programs. The committee should also be charged to develop program services across the K–12 spectrum, and it should include representation from all levels.

Many committees started programs at the elementary level only and then experienced conflicts in trying to extend the program to the middle school and high school levels. Articulation of program services across all three levels is necessary to assure that gifted youth have a continuity of special experiences to foster their talents during all the school years.

THE MODEL

The authors of this book have spent hundreds of hours discussing the characteristics and needs of gifted youth and the concepts and program models set forth in this book. These discussions were carried on over $2^{1}\!/_2$ years. We concluded that a reconceptualization of the field of gifted education and a more powerful and substantive approach were needed. We perceive gifted youth as needing daily, challenging learning experiences. Much more is required than the ubiquitous but limited pullout program.

Assertions

First and foremost, we assert that programs for the gifted and talented must address lofty goals and be oriented to a striving for excellence on the part of both teachers and students. Second, we believe that curriculum for the gifted and talented should be based in the traditional disciplines, and conceptually oriented. The latter implies that the curriculum is to focus on concepts, principles, issues, themes, and ideas rather than rules, facts, basic skills. Third, instruction for the gifted and talented should be a "generative" process in which the students are actively engaged in solving problems, inquiring, discovering, experimenting, seeking understanding, and creating their own conceptual systems.

The Nature of Giftedness

We have also addressed the question of the nature of giftedness and the correlated question of how to assess it. We conclude that four major psychological components comprise giftedness: (1) superior talent and/or ability, (2) a high degree of motivation, (3) unique self-concept and perceptual characteristics, and (4) high-level creative capacities. Talents and abilities are diverse, ranging from the academic and artistic to the social and vocational. Some abilities, such as those in mathematics or verbal areas, can be assessed reliably with pencil-and-paper tests, but talents in the arts, leadership, or vocational areas can be best assessed by observing performance in realistic learning situations or by evaluating products.

Motivation in the gifted and talented shows itself in depth of interest, task persistence, exploratory reading, efforts to excel, a competitive spirit, and devotion to study within a discipline. Single-mindedness of purpose and relentless pursuit of understanding also seem to be recurrent characteristics of the gifted. Intrinsic motivation, which grows out of love for learning in itself rather than payoffs or rewards (extrinsic motivation), characterizes the gifted and talented. Motivation is a component that we expect to be fostered in programs for the gifted and talented, but at any point when it is assessed, it is also an excellent predictor of the future motivational character of a gifted youth.

Self-concept is another critical component of giftedness and talent. The self-concept is not ordinarily quantified as high or low but, rather, it is assessed in terms of *positiveness* of the self view in general or of the academic self view. For the gifted and talented, a positive self view is needed in relation to academic ability and potential achievement in the talent area. *Realism* of the self view is also essential. Gifted and talented youth should accurately perceive their abilities and not over- or underestimate it. Consistency between the self view and ability produces a psychological state of harmony in which gifted youth can develop their talents in the absence of debilitating internal conflicts.

Closely related to the self-concept is the *perceptual field* of the gifted and talented. Breadth and openness should characterize the gifted and talented. Their view of the world, school, learning, and studies should be global and interdisciplinary. Their studies should help them perceive the interrelatedness of fields.

Finally, there is the creative component. This is the capacity related both to certain abilities and a set of personality characteristics. Creative people are able to use the divergent thinking abilities of fluency, flexibility, originality, and elaboration, as well as general problem solving skills. They also have developed the personal traits of independence, risk taking, humor, playfulness, internal orientation, and problem sensing. Through the creativity component, in concert with ability/talent, self-concept and motivation, gifted people are able to associate and synthesize and thereby produce new ideas or products.

The Ideal Program

The ideal program for the gifted at the elementary level is the full-time or self-contained model, at least for all the basic academic subjects. These programs can afford opportunities for continuous, fast-paced progress in mathematics, science, language arts, and social studies, as well as a variety of enrichment opportunities. Gifted children in these programs can be mainstreamed in physical education, art, and music to provide opportunities for social interaction with average and less able children.

At the secondary level gifted youth should have opportunities for accelerated learning in all the basic disciplines, through honors classes, seminars, Advanced Placement classes, foreign languages, and supplementary enrichment opportunities. A major approach to identification of the gifted and to assessment of their specific academic needs is now available through the regional talent searches offered all over the United States and the off-grade testing offered with the *Scholastic Aptitude Test.*

We are in the early stages of a new era in education. In this new era the schools will endeavor to provide the best possible education for *all* youth. The new education will address the special needs of youth and help them achieve their highest potential. Better education of the gifted and talented will benefit our nation as a whole by rearing a new generation of professionals, artists, managers, inventors, and politicians who will provide the creativity our country needs to maintain its position as world leader.

Index